Praise for *Inside the Minds*

"A tremendous resource, amalgamating commentary from leading professionals that is presented in a concise, easy to read format." – Alan H. Aronson, Shareholder, Akerman Senterfitt

"Aspatore's *Inside the Minds* series allows strategic professionals to access cutting-edge information from proven experts in the field. Their approach of providing consolidated, valuable, current information reflects their true understanding of the life of an executive. We need the best information in the most concise format. Aspatore is a consistently reliable resource that provides great information without expending unnecessary time." – Kimberly L. Giangrande, Principal, Intuitive HR

"A terrific compilation of real world, successful strategies and practical advice." – Sig Anderman, CEO, Ellie Mae Inc.

"Must read source for leaders wanting to stay ahead of emerging best practices and to understand the thought processes leading up to the innovation." – Mark Gasta, SVP and Chief Human Resources Officer, Vail Resorts Management Company

"A refreshing collection of strategic insights, not dreary commonplaces, from some of the best of the profession." – Roger J. Magnuson, Partner, Dorsey & Whitney LLP

"Unique and insightful perspectives. Great to read and an excellent way to stay in touch. – Filippo Passerini, President of Global Business Services and CIO, The Procter & Gamble Company

"A must read for C-level and senior executives. The information is based on actual experiences from successful senior leaders and has real, practical value presented in a very useable format." – Stephen Fugale, VP and CIO, Villanova University

"Some of the best insight around from sources in the know" – Donald R. Kirk, Shareholder, Fowler White Boggs PA

"Powerful insight from people who practice every day!" – Andrea R. Bortner, VP, GCSD Human Resources, Harris Corporation

"Aspatore's *Inside the Minds* series provides practical, cutting edge advice from those with insight into the real world challenges that confront businesses in the global economy." – Michael Bednarek, Partner, Shearman & Sterling LLP

"Outstanding insights from respected business leaders." – R. Scot Sellers, CEO, Archstone

ASPATORE

Aspatore Books, a Thomson Reuters business, exclusively publishes C-Level executives and partners from the world's most respected companies and law firms. Each publication provides professionals of all levels with proven business and legal intelligence from industry insiders—direct and unfiltered insight from those who know it best. Aspatore Books is committed to publishing an innovative line of business and legal titles that lay forth principles and offer insights that can have a direct financial impact on the reader's business objectives.

Each chapter in the *Inside the Minds* series offers thought leadership and expert analysis on an industry, profession, or topic, providing a future-oriented perspective and proven strategies for success. Each author has been selected based on their experience and C-Level standing within the business and legal communities. *Inside the Minds* was conceived to give a first-hand look into the leading minds of top business executives and lawyers worldwide, presenting an unprecedented collection of views on various industries and professions.

CONTENTS

Ed Rodriguez   7
VP, Field Human Resources, Ventura Foods
LEVERAGING VENTURA'S EDGE: FIVE STEPS TO
BUILDING POSITIVE EMPLOYEE RELATIONS

Bill Streitberger   17
VP, Human Resources, Red Robin International
EMPLOYEE RELATIONS MANAGEMENT IN A
DIVERSE ORGANIZATION

Jennie Fotovich   27
VP, Human Resources, Roche Bros. Supermarkets
RESPECT, COMMUNICATION, WORKFORCE
DEVELOPMENT: A PROVEN MODEL

Trina Maynes   39
SVP, Human Resources, Nickelodeon
PARTNERING WITH LEADERSHIP TO MANAGE
EMPLOYEE MORALE AND PRODUCTIVITY IN A
GLOBAL, COMPLEX, AND INNOVATIVE CULTURAL
ENVIRONMENT

Keith A. Chrzanowski   47
SVP, Global Human Resources, Given Imaging
MAXIMIZING EMPLOYEE ENGAGEMENT
FROM POINT OF HIRE

Brenda Rogers   57
VP, Human Resources, Roku Inc.
STRATEGIC BUSINESS DRIVERS FOR
HIGH-PERFORMING PEOPLE PRACTICES

Barry Hartunian 67
Chief Talent Officer and VP, Human Resources
Communispace
EFFECTIVE GLOBAL HR AND BUSINESS LEADERSHIP

Greg Kayata 77
VP, Total Rewards, Covidien
NAVIGATING EMPLOYEE RELATIONS ISSUES DURING ORGANIZATIONAL TRANSFORMATION

Lyle Mark Daugherty 87
VP, Human Resources, Ancra Group Companies
DRIVING COMPANY GOALS THROUGH A FOCUSED EMPLOYEE RELATIONS STRATEGY

Melissa Dunn 97
Global Director, Human Resources
Thermo Fisher Scientific
MANAGING GENERATIONAL AND CULTURAL EMPLOYEE RELATIONSHIPS

Kelley Berlin 109
SVP, Human Resources, SymphonyIRI Group
TAILORING THE RIGHT EMPLOYEE ENGAGEMENT STRATEGY FOR YOUR ORGANIZATION

Leveraging Ventura's Edge: Five Steps to Building Positive Employee Relations

Ed Rodriguez
Vice President, Field Human Resources
Ventura Foods

ASPATORE

Introduction

The traditional business case for positive employee relations has typically been based on risk management factors like lawsuit avoidance and less tangible benefits such as "increased productivity and efficiency," which are much harder to measure. In non-union settings, leveraging positive employee relations to maintain non-union status has also been a principal argument. However, there is an opportunity to expand the business case for positive employee relations and to link it to broader organizational and strategic imperatives; doing so will facilitate and accelerate efforts to build an organizational climate that attracts and retains key talent at all levels, and ultimately ensures the long-term success of the enterprise. Whether you work in a small or large company, attempting to drive positive employee relations at a local level, in a vacuum, or in a fashion that is not clearly connected to a solid business case can be limiting and unsustainable.

Especially in a small- to mid-sized organization with fewer levels, a flatter structure and less divisional complexity, and where leadership alignment and "speed to market" can be leveraged, the opportunity to implement organizational change that redefines and repositions the value of positive employee relations can be uniquely exciting. I recently made a career change from a large $60 billion multinational corporation with close to 300,000 employees worldwide and a well-established, highly respected, and strategically focused HR function (and organizational culture), to a smaller domestic company with 2,600 employees, where HR had historically been viewed as "traditional" or "transactional." My experience in just over a year with my new company has been a case study in HR's role in driving organizational change and cultural transformation. One of the changes involves repositioning the purpose, benefits, and overall value of positive employee relations with respect to our company's growth plans.

Aligning Positive Employee Relations Strategy in an Evolving Organization

Ventura Foods LLC is a joint venture between Mitsui and CHS that was established in 1996. Ventura Foods is a successful company that has grown from $500 million to over $2.5 billion in revenue, primarily through a series of acquisitions over the past sixteen years. The company was built around an operational focus on cost, service, quality, and safety, and had been led under a fairly decentralized structure with each of its eleven manufacturing plants—producing a combination of foodservice and retail dressings, spreads, shortening, mayonnaise, retail oils, and other food products—operating as independent and autonomous "divisions."

Ventura Foods has a positive reputation in its business segment as a low-cost producer, flexible partner, and quality supplier. A sound business model, a tenured and stable workforce with company turnover in the single digits, and strong technical expertise have enabled Ventura Foods to recently experience two of the most profitable years in its history, even in the midst of a challenging foodservice and retail economy.

Although neither the company nor the "business model" was broken, Ventura Foods' owners were looking to accelerate growth. A new CEO, Chris Furman, recently joined the company and made it clear that he did not join an organization in need of a "turnaround"—his vision was to take Ventura Foods to the next level of performance through organic growth, domestic acquisitions, brand extensions, and international expansion in the years ahead. One of the tangible business goals he established was to double net income in the next five years.

Given these goals, we have focused on five critical elements to build a positive employee relations strategy in the context of our new direction:

1. Securing executive sponsorship and engagement
2. Linking key HR initiatives to the corporate strategy and vision
3. Influencing key line stakeholders with a business case/ROI mentality
4. Balancing between "push" and "pull" approaches
5. Building "Level 3" HR capability

Securing Executive Sponsorship and Engagement

To truly be successful in delivering a positive employee relations strategy, senior leaders must view HR as an enabler. Our new CEO inherited a tactically and technically talented organization with a "whatever it takes" attitude toward cost, quality, and service. His desire was to build on that foundation with a corporate business strategy and vision that would guide our interactions with customers, suppliers, and each other. His goal was to reinforce the notion that Ventura Foods employees were "part of something special."

HR played a key role in our corporate identity initiative. Employees at every level of our organization were engaged to shape, define, and refine our core values, mission, and vision through a series of interviews, focus groups, and pilots over the course of several months. Our new company vision, "The Ventura Edge," was rolled out, along with a new and aligned corporate business strategy at a national meeting with corporate and field leaders from every function. The hallmark of this new vision was the identification and alignment around our company's signature strength, "agility," which defines who we are and our interactional approach internally and externally. "The Ventura Edge" is being rolled out to every employee in the company using an interactive "discovery map" engagement process, and will be woven into the fabric of our employee engagement, talent development, and organizational capability processes moving forward.

The importance of the people agenda was reinforced by the inclusion of "Growing our People" as one of the four key platforms of our new strategic plan—and by the fact that employee satisfaction, as measured by our Redesigned Organizational Health Survey, was one of the key success measures. From a company vision standpoint, our core competencies include an "investment in a learning organization that results in expertise and growth of our people." In addition to the core values that guide our actions, the people and cultural implications of our core competencies reflect the strengths we leverage today as well as the aspirational expectations of the company we are looking to become over time.

Establishing this broad and aspirational vision created a common language, purpose, and direction, which was foundational in building our employee relations strategy. Having a seat (and more importantly a voice) at the table translated into HR being included as a "platform and not just an enabler" to support our future growth and to help build a culture that would reinforce next-level performance. The new corporate vision was a leader-led, leader-guided initiative that established new expectations for leaders and sent a resounding message around the company's current and future investment in people, communication, engagement, and learning.

Linking Key HR Initiatives to the Corporate Strategy and Vision

HR strategy should be fundamentally linked to the business strategy and company vision. Aligning specific employee relations initiatives to the strategy and vision accelerates the acceptance, implementation, and sustainability of these initiatives in support of broader organizational goals.

One of the key employee relations initiatives that encompassed many of the principles contained in the new vision was our frontline development process. The four main elements of the program included the implementation of quarterly all-employee "State of the Business" meetings, weekly tailgate shift meetings, individual frontline coaching and development sessions, and DDI-based leadership training for all location leaders. The foundation of the program was to create "points of interaction" to regularly and proactively engage frontline employees in issue identification and resolution, relationship building, personal growth and development, and to build a stronger connection to location specific and companywide news, updates, and information. The program was developed and piloted in our St. Joseph, Missouri plant, and is being rolled out throughout the company this year.

For many leaders (and employees) this level of engagement was new and different; employees expressed appreciation via focus group feedback sessions for the authentic and genuine efforts of their supervisors and location leaders to connect with them at a different level. From an operations leadership perspective, linking these efforts to key manufacturing initiatives like Lean Manufacturing and its principles, which focus on teamwork, respect for others, and employee engagement as organizational enablers to enhancing customer value and achieving efficiencies through continuous improvement, was critical.

In addition to frontline development, a number of performance-based and talent-based initiatives have been launched to support our business strategy and mission. Our redesigned organizational health survey has questions that are linked to our new company vision, and the results will be used to measure employee satisfaction on our new strategic framework. A new, fully automated talent acquisition system was implemented, which will not only streamline the application, hiring, and onboarding process, but will also bolster Ventura Foods' branding efforts as we seek to elevate our efforts to become a destination for key talent. Ventura Foods is also in the process of developing a companywide and cross-functional learning and development strategy that will be the foundation for organizational and individual capability building efforts in support of our desire to become a true learning organization.

All of these initiatives are aligned with our corporate strategy, company vision, and the operational needs of the business.

Influencing Key Line Stakeholders with a Business Case/ROI Mentality

It is not enough to say "the CEO says it is important." As influence leaders, HR professionals need to focus on influencing managers to invest in new tools and new thinking based on a sound business case and a return on investment approach. Especially in a low margin, lowest cost producer environment, employees and leaders will view (and question) the opportunity cost of any new program or initiative that pulls them away, at least in the short term, from focusing on cost, quality, and productivity.

The time and energy that was invested in executing Ventura Foods' first Succession Planning process across field and corporate operations was driven by two main ROI factors. First, it became clear to senior operations leaders that we did not have the internal depth and bench strength to replace key leaders who were nearing retirement age in the months and years ahead. Identifying internal high-potential and promotable talent, investing in individual development plans, and developing external recruiting strategies that would address specific gaps became a business, and not just an organizational, imperative. Second, as we experienced unexpected churn in what had previously been a fairly stable senior leader group, the costs of turnover highlighted the need to balance talent acquisition with internal talent development. While different organizations have several methodologies of calculating and accounting for the "cost of turnover," it becomes clear and tangible the moment the recruiter fees, relocation invoices, and other exit/hiring costs appear, and the inevitable game of "hot potato" ensues to determine who and how the charges will be processed, assigned, and/or budgeted.

Similarly, an analysis of our frontline turnover demonstrated that a large percentage of our turnover was driven by employees leaving in the first three years of employment. The business case for our investment in a new talent acquisition system, which included better online capabilities, enhanced company branding efforts, and better tools for onboarding new employees, was built around the need to attract, hire, and train new hires in a more streamlined and effective manner.

Finally, it is important to ensure that solutions are not overcomplicated, over-engineered or administratively overwhelming, but are instead laser focused on addressing real and tangible business needs. Managers with multiple priorities and no surplus of time will often think, if not ask, "What is the effort versus the return?" Consequently, it is critical to keep things simple and to avoid HR "geek speak." Leaders are looking for business partners who understand the needs of the company, speak their language, and are tuned into "what keeps them up at night" (profitability, controllable costs, customer service, quality, etc.)—they do not want to hear about ideas or theories that sound like cookie-cutter solutions or best practice templates that came out of the latest organizational development textbook.

Balancing Between Push and Pull

In a small- to mid-sized company, enterprise-wide people systems and programs may not be broadly implemented or institutionalized, so it is important to avoid overwhelming the organization with too many new HR tools, initiatives, and programs too quickly. The key is to set the right pace and sequence of programs and to be sensitive to "peak season" business activity, customer selling cycles, and operational calendars.

Leading change can sometimes require "pushing" a lot of change to the organization. Our new performance management process, which includes objective setting, regular one-on-one meetings, midyear reviews, and end-of-year performance evaluations, was launched and implemented in less than a year. Establishing a performance baseline for all exempt employees against a new set of performance standards and expectations was foundational based on the company's plans to grow and expand both organically and through acquisition.

There are going to be certain circumstances, such as the example mentioned above, where a push approach is necessary; however, creating organizational and leadership "pull" is an ideal way to align key initiatives. Establishing the business case and identifying the organizational gap, and allowing for grassroots input and feedback to help shape, develop, and pilot programs usually results in a credible, validated, and sponsored initiative. This approach ensures you "bring others with you" from an operational standpoint.

The frontline development program referenced earlier is an example of a pull-driven initiative. In light of the historical lack of investment in structured training and formal/informal communication channels, our senior operations leaders understood the need and potential value for investing in supervisor capability and employee engagement efforts to build on a strong connection with our hourly employees. Leader-led sponsorship from the top both facilitated and accelerated buy-in at the middle management and supervisory levels of the organization.

Building "Level 3" HR Capability

Having a credible, aligned, and effective HR organization at a corporate and field level is critical. HR has to prove it is connected to the people and understands the business. Becoming operationally savvy, building greater financial literacy, or making it a priority to create visibility at unexpected times and unexpected places builds intimacy, trust, and familiarity. Simply asking to be involved in business, departmental, or operational meetings with a genuine and authentic interest in improving business knowledge is typically viewed in a positive light.

Level 1 HR can be described as traditional, transactional, or service-oriented HR. Level 2 HR can be described as having greater involvement in the business and operations and a greater involvement in strategic and systemic solutions to broader organizational challenges. Level 3 HR is becoming a true business partner and trusted advisor to your senior leaders, a valued internal coach and resource to management peers, and a respected and engaged leader to your frontline employees, with clear alignment with the business and the culture.

Creating and aligning an HR plan with primary line partners is an ideal way to build Level 3 business partnership. These plans typically include a fact-based assessment of organizational strengths and opportunities, the top three to five organizational priorities, and specific action plans to close and/or address key gaps. These HR plans are also an excellent vehicle to identify and pre-wire innovative solutions or "above and beyond" thinking and ideas.

Developing "breakroom to boardroom" organizational visibility and savvy can accelerate an HR professional's role as a change leader. HR, based on its broad and cross-functional line of sight within an organization, is in a unique position to leverage change leadership skills to drive employee relations initiatives that support broader organizational and strategic objectives.

Conclusion

"Connecting the dots" between employee relations programs and a broader corporate strategy and company vision ensures short-term and long-term success. Making sure that a sound business case accompanies any change or new initiative and that a "keep it simple" approach is utilized to create momentum and pull are key to short-term and long-term success.

The five steps above may not specifically apply to every unique circumstance, but the concepts and frameworks can be useful in planning any broad-based employee relations strategy. Utilizing a company vision and strategy as a "validation screen" for employee engagement programs and initiatives will help ensure proper alignment, support, and sustainability.

Key Takeaways

- Creating short-term and long-term success requires a link between specific employee relations programs and a broader corporate strategy.
- Avoid implementing "textbook solutions" and overwhelming the company with new "HR" tools, initiatives, and programs, particularly in a small- to mid-size setting where formalized implementations may not yet be in place.
- Increase HR credibility and influence through visibility, knowing the business, and increasing financial literacy.

Ed Rodriguez joined Ventura Foods as vice president of field human resources in 2011. He began his career in human resources at PepsiCo in 1995. After serving as a human resources manager in several Los Angeles area locations, he became regional staffing and training manager for Southern California in 1999. In 2001, he joined Pepsi Bottling Group's headquarters HR team as a labor relations manager and chief spokesperson. A year later, he joined the acquisition and integration team, and later was named director of human resources for PBG Mexico, where he was responsible for 26,000 employees, twenty-five plants, and more than 150 sales and distribution locations. In 2004, Mr. Rodriguez returned to PBG's headquarters as vice president of international capability for its Mexico, Canada, and European operations, and was later named vice president of Organizational Capability and Diversity, where he led PBG to a #2 ranking on DiversityInc Magazine's 2006 Top Companies for Diversity. In 2007, he was named divisional vice president of Pepsi's West Business Unit, where he was responsible for 7,500 employees across California, Oregon, Washington, Nevada, Hawaii, and Alaska. In 2009, Mr. Rodriguez was named to HispanicBusiness magazine's Top 60 Corporate Elite list.

Mr. Rodriguez earned a bachelor's degree in English from UC Santa Barbara and a master's degree in communication management from USC. He is currently pursuing a PhD in educational studies with an emphasis on leadership development at Chapman University in Orange County, California.

Employee Relations Management in a Diverse Organization

Bill Streitberger
Vice President, Human Resources
Red Robin International

ASPATORE

Introduction

Red Robin is a national, publicly traded casual dining chain that operates in forty-two states and employs 20,000 team members. The role of HR is to serve as a business partner, not only for the individual operators, but for the other executives as well, and provide guidance on compliance issues and effective employee relations management.

Employee relations involves many programs, communication channels, rules, guidelines, and culture maintenance; a strong employee relations strategy also helps resolve issues in the workplace, whether in the individual restaurants or in the corporate office. It also involves developing policies for the interviewing process, recruitment, compensation, terminations, disciplinary actions, and just the general rules of the road. In our case, we have three HR directors located in different regions across the company with supporting generalists who collectively pinpoint and develop effective solutions that will help support our enterprise objective of growing the organization through our people.

Developing and maintaining our employee relations strategies originates with the HR team, but we work closely with our legal team since the rules and regulations can vary widely from state to state. We also work very closely with our operations team, since they can help us determine where we need to adopt, train, and develop based on what they are seeing in the actual restaurants. Finally, on the staffing end, we work with the marketing team to create internal branding strategies that help keep the organization aligned. In an organization of our size, with people spread out over forty-two states, maintaining consistent communication with managers and team members can be a challenge. Therefore, it is important to ensure we have the appropriate workforce policies in place to effectively communicate and address all of our employee relations issues.

The Effect of Employee Relations Management on Culture

Maintaining positive employee relations has an important effect on the culture and the overall well-being of the organization. If employees are satisfied with the company, they will be much more productive and more engaged in creating a positive experience for our guests. A positive guest experience, in turn, means higher sales and a healthy organization. Our company is a service-oriented organization that promises a positive, personable experience for our guests, so we need to ensure that we are attracting the right employees who are excited to create an engaging experience for our guests. This relationship is the core of our business; it is what drives sales and enables us to continue growing and creating new opportunities.

Because the guest experience is so critical to our business model, it is of course important that we hire individuals who possess a positive outlook, but we also need to set the tone for these expectations through our organization's culture. Doing so allows us to clearly communicate our expectations to our employees and really just set the guardrails for the day-to-day duties of running a shift, preparing food, taking care of guests, making drinks, and so on. There are no secrets here; we believe in cultural transparency because it helps everyone understand what we need from them and how we will reward them for that service.

Important Skills for Effective Employee Relations Management

When it comes to employee relations, remember that there are usually four sides to every story. Employees who are engaged in employee relations issues must possess plenty of patience and the ability to listen. Additionally, they need to have a strong understanding of local state and federal guidelines, particularly concerning employment laws. Individuals need to know how to apply the necessary resources to resolve a particular situation.

Investigations that are made anonymously are challenging and require quite a bit of patience in particular because you are unable to dig down into specific circumstances with an unknown individual. To truly delve into the issue, you need to cast a wider net and involve a range of individuals. However, when an inquiry is made, individuals tend to get nervous, because everyone truly wants to do the right thing. In situations like these, it is just a matter of taking the time to speak with a number of people, maintain confidentialities, and above all else, listen. If a situation arises, you are likely to hear several variations of an incident, and at the end of the day, it is all about finding the best possible outcome to the problem.

We also provide training modules, both online and in person, to prepare to effectively address any employee issues that may arise. Essentially we walk them through the basics—what they need to do to be productive, what they need to listen for, what rules and policies exist, and how to engage in communications and deliver feedback. The training teaches them how to address an issue and how to document it if needed, but we also help them determine when it is time to pick up the phone and call HR. Most of the time, employee relations is about individual conversations with team members, but there is always the possibility that extra support will be required; we encourage managers to bring us into the situation sooner rather than later, which is all part of that training.

We also offer various educational programs on sexual harassment, discrimination, and other policy related behaviors of our business, so we have a wide variety of methods to help us communicate our policies and procedures. The in-class training sessions are also effective, because they provide managers with the opportunity to ask us questions. During these sessions, they will usually pose various hypothetical situations, asking what they should say if something should happen, so we will walk through the situations together and help them learn to address these specific cases while understanding the thought process behind it.

Managing Diversity, Inclusion, and Generational Differences in the Workplace

Our organization is presently developing educational programs to address diversity and inclusion, and we still have a bit of progress to make before we are ready for a rollout. In addition to training programs, I think it is important to realize that diversity all begins with staffing. We cast a wide net when filling our positions so we can bring many backgrounds into our workforce and encourage diversity in a very natural, organic way. However, it is also important to teach the philosophy of inclusion; everyone has something to offer, so it is important to be mindful and encourage that in the workplace. We will be working on developing these educational tools while being mindful of cultural sensitivities in our methods. There are so many approaches out there, so we want to make sure we are careful in choosing a method that works with our organization and our culture.

Additionally, managing different generations in the workforce can certainly be a challenging aspect when it comes to employee relations. In our organization, a front door hostess who helps seat guests can be as young as eighteen years old, while our managers are usually more of the baby boomer generation. There is a pretty wide gap in age there, so it is important to understand that the younger generation might have a completely different outlook. The managers might expect that if they tell you to do something, you will do it; however, younger employees tend to want to know why—which is not a bad thing—but it is a difference in communication and training.

As a general rule of thumb, however, employee needs and expectations depend on the circumstances associated with a particular individual rather than generational trends. For example, we have some employees who are in college, so we need to be mindful and provide flexibility in their schedules for exams, classes, and so forth. We also have young parents who need flexibility for child care, school, and other needs. We have a diverse range of age groups that all have different expectations, so we just need to balance flexibility with the needs of the business. We explain the importance of balancing these needs with individual accommodations, and we try to do so, first and foremost, based on performance, but also by understanding and doing our best to accommodate when possible.

As a restaurant and hospitality organization, we tend to be the busiest when people are out of work—nights, weekends, and holidays. We understand that employees have families and want to participate in events that will likely take place during our peak times, so it is all about creating balance. Some of our employees choose to be with their families during the holidays; some employees are single and do not mind picking up those shifts. There always has to be some give and take because it is impossible to accommodate everyone all of the time, but we do our best to balance shifts as much as possible.

Talent Development and Career Training

Our talent development opportunities are always evolving; however, we generally start by bringing in the best talent we can into a position and then monitor their performance based on the needs of both the business and the individual. Then we will make adjustments as needed. For example, if we have a talented manager who could use some more development in their organizational capabilities or communication skills, we can provide them with training, whether it be a module we have in-house or an outside seminar. We work with individuals in a variety of ways based on their personal needs to help them develop in their career. This is something that is constantly evolving particularly with the development of technology. In the past, everything had to be done face to face; so much can be done online today, so we are always looking to see what tools are available to help develop our workforce.

Addressing Delicate Situations

Sometimes employee relations management can involve delicate situations, and in the case of an anonymous incident, we truly do our best to maintain confidentialities. We cannot make any guarantees given that we are speaking with so many individuals to get to the root of an issue. We can, however, guarantee no retaliation; we appreciate when people step forward to let us know something is amiss. We document the incident and ask individuals not to discuss it with anyone but us to keep rumors at a minimum. People usually understand that we are serious about finding a solution, but we are not on a witch hunt. Sometimes the issue has to do with two people who do not get along, and sometimes it is something more personal, so it is HR's experience that comes into play in solving the issue delicately, quickly, and professionally.

Monitoring Employee Morale

We use an online engagement survey to measure employee morale levels in the organization, specifically in terms of satisfaction with the organization, training, their supervisor, and things of that nature. We monitor these results by individual restaurants as well as the organization as a whole, and we analyze whether there are certain trends in a particular region or restaurant we should be aware of. We use a scale of one to five, five being the highest, and these rankings help us assess how employees feel working for our company. If we see a lower score, we will delve deeper via focus groups to find out more about these concerns. If a new supervisor is holding employees more accountable, that might not be a bad thing for us;

however, if we find that someone has gone off the path a bit, it gives us the opportunity to work with the manager in question and correct the issue.

We measure this engagement on an annual basis, which also includes the input of our exempt staff and managers in the home office. Additionally, we perform exit interviews and combine these results on a quarterly basis to tie it back to any existing incident studies. If turnover spikes in correlation with a particular incident report, we can identify where the issues exist and correct them so they do not continue to be an issue.

New Directions When Hiring Talent

We are also deploying a new paperless selection process for new hires, and all of our applications, whether corporate, management, or restaurant staff, will go through this central location. When people enter the site, they can view information such as our benefits and opportunities, and there is even a 3D model of the restaurant floor. We have introduced this process to better reflect the preferred methods of communication in the younger generations. The job search takes place online these days, and it is helpful to us to screen candidates through this online assessment and then communicate back to the hiring manager. The micro-site is very high technology, and that leads to our applicant tracking system, which is not so new, and then it feeds into the hiring process. This is something of which we are extremely proud. Last year, under our old system, we were only getting 40,000 hits a month. However, in January alone, under our new system, we have hit 250,000 hits a month! This confirms that this is how the new generation prefers to do things, so we make it easier for them, but quite frankly, it is also a lot easier on our managers as well.

Conclusion

The ability to listen is the most important component when managing employee relations. When individuals are thinking about what they are going to say next and trying to fit as much as they can into a conversation, they are not listening well. Moreover, it is important to stay objective, and that is always a challenge. You might have to investigate someone that you hold in high esteem, and if you believe that it is going to be an issue, it is advisable to ask someone else to step in to maintain that objective point of view. If you are not objective, you are bound to make mistakes.

For upcoming HR professionals, it is important to assess career goals. If someone is interested in working with employee relations, they need to make sure they have the right level of education from a legislative standpoint. They need to be willing to continue updating their education with the understanding that these rules and regulations change all the time. It is also about having patience and the desire to help people. Employee relations, like everything else, is not for everyone. Managing these issues can certainly be challenging and time consuming, but it is also very rewarding.

Key Takeaways

- Always remember that there are four sides to every story, and it will take plenty of patience and listening to unravel the core issue.
- HR professionals who are involved in employee relations management should have a strong handle on various rules and regulations to effectively address a potential situation.
- Monitoring employee engagement and then analyzing trends is a useful way to identify any recurring issues in the workforce. Once a trend has been identified, the issue can be explored and then corrected.
- When it comes to employee relations, listening is the most important factor. If you are trying to plan how you are filling the conversation, then you are not listening well.

Bill Streitberger is vice president of human resources at Red Robin International. In September 2008, Mr. Streitberger joined the leadership team of Red Robin Gourmet Burgers, a 400-plus unit public restaurant chain, to build the capability to deliver superior results. Mr. Streitberger is a business leader with expertise in managing organizational and human resources processes that drive bottom-line results. His areas of expertise focus on creating organizational capability and stability and developing high levels of employee commitment and loyalty along with achieving results from shareholders, team members, and guests.

As vice president of human resources, Mr. Streitberger oversees the day-to-day functions for all areas of human resources. He believes it is important to organize and utilize key strategies and procedures to build the foundation for the entire human resources function. Mr. Streitberger has implemented and refined systems and administrative procedures throughout the company with an emphasis on benefits, compensation, recruiting, and employee relations.

With more than twenty-five years of experience in the human resources field, Mr. Streitberger has directed human resources and recruiting functions at numerous restaurant chains including BJ's Restaurants, The Cheesecake Factory, and Brinker International. He is a graduate of University of Central Florida and currently resides in Denver, Colorado.

Respect, Communication, Workforce Development: A Proven Model

Jennie Fotovich
Vice President, Human Resources
Roche Bros. Supermarkets

ASPATORE

Introduction

I have always considered myself a very fortunate individual and my career has been an exciting journey that has enabled me to be a part of many terrific organizations. While I was initially involved in the restaurant industry, I made the transition to grocery approximately twenty years ago. Having held numerous leadership positions in more than one industry has allowed me to gain tremendous insight into associate relations and how to assist managers in achieving optimal performance through others.

When I was approached and asked to share some of my experiences in the form of a chapter, it was a challenge to narrow the topic to one small segment of HR. I hope that many of the processes and thoughts that I share will help others in their quest to build stronger teams.

My current role is vice president of human resources for Roche Bros. Supermarkets in Massachusetts.

Redefining Roles and Responsibilities

Redefining roles and responsibilities is easier said than done and anyone who has had a consultant or outside party review work models understands this challenge. After six months of reviewing the HR department at Roche, it was apparent to me that each staff position needed to be clearly defined. Under my direct supervision, job descriptions were written outlining the minimum requirements, duties, and responsibilities for all job positions. Several HR staff members exhibited specific talents that could be better utilized if given additional training and empowered to be held accountable for that area of the department. One example would be an individual with a gift for understanding and helping associates or handling customer complaints that come into the department. Consequently, that individual now serves as the department liaison for all worker's compensation and general liability claims. I have another individual who has recently completed their master's degree in human resources. This associate demonstrated tremendous talent and legal knowledge regarding HR in general. This person has since become an HR field representative responsible for associate relations and field investigations. Additionally, I have another staff member who is exceptionally detail oriented and is now responsible for all internal filing, computer processing, I-9 auditing, DOL compliance, etc. This does not summarize the entire staff and all their areas of accountability; it simply demonstrates a method of defining roles and responsibilities.

Prior to my arrival, the HR staff would attempt to address questions, or issues, from associates individually. There were cases when an associate's call would be transferred two or three times in an effort to reach the correct individual that could resolve their problem. After their roles were defined, this was published and sent to our retail locations, which provided our associates the ability to contact the correct resource.

Once this was accomplished, each staff member received development and education to the extent that they are now considered a subject matter expert in their realm of expertise. This restructuring of the HR department streamlined our process and enabled my staff to add value to their roles.

Completing the changes discussed above has had a cumulative effect of enabling our department to provide added value to the company. We are no longer considered just the *Personnel Department* that pushes paper and handles the service award dinner or family day outing. Now the HR department is considered a company resource. If a member of management requests assistance with coaching, mentoring, motivational techniques, promotional requirements or soft skills training they seek our assistance. They utilize HR as the strategic partner that every great organization needs.

In a nutshell, our HR department has experienced an amazing transformation in the last three years. While we have experienced many bumps and bruises along the way, I am very proud of the result.

RSTO: A Model for Employee Relations Management

At Roche Bros, employee relations management can be summed up in an acronym that is posted on the wall in every store: RSTO – Respect, Support, and Totally Team Oriented. It promotes and cultivates maintaining a mutual respect for everyone—not just for our customers but also for each other. Our culture is to live by the golden rule: always treat others as you would like to be treated.

These values affect our company's culture and overall health tremendously. In my position with four major grocers, I have seen different acronyms but have never been part of an organization that truly reflected their own acronym the way that Roche Bros does with RSTO. I believe that the deep engagement of its associates is because the owners, our president, and other executives are so involved with the day-to-day operations. They are out there continuously encouraging everyone to just take care of the customer, regardless of what it may cost the company. Our number one focus is to take care of the customer and take care of each other. The rest of it will follow.

This has been the guiding principle for the success of the organization and this year we will celebrate our sixtieth anniversary. The owners have literally built a multi-million dollar organization on the principle of respecting everyone and being involved in the community.

HR's Role in Employee Relations and Workforce Development

The HR department and our operations team are jointly involved in developing and maintaining employee relations. The operations team is responsible for the activities and results of our 4,000-plus associates in eighteen retail locations. This includes approximately 200 managers or assistant managers in multiple departments.

Coaching others through the delicate process of managing associates' performance is probably the most impactful task that I am involved in on a regular basis. As a best practice, we search for opportunities to recognize good performance, and while we continually strive to recognize our associates in a positive manner, we occasionally spend more time addressing our underperforming associates. In many work environments, you frequently have associates who may not always be up to the company's standards or not performing their job correctly. When it comes to maintaining good employee relations, the method of addressing performance correctly is critical.

We prepare managers to effectively and consistently address employee relations issues through coaching, teaching, and training both on-site and via e-mails. If requested, a knowledgeable HR staff member will go on-site as an observer and give managers feedback on how well they did so that they may improve with each occurrence. Managers are encouraged to send us documentation on counseling forms so that we may review it with them and assist with any changes that need to be made. This not only provides for coaching opportunities, it also aids in protecting the company.

Training is imperative for all layers in an organization whose multiple levels of associates serve the public. Showing respect to everyone is critical to business growth and/or maintaining your status in this economy. At times this may be more challenging when you employ many different generations of associates. The training may need to be provided in multiple methods so that each generation understands their role in the organization.

Managers are coached through the entire process. This includes compiling documentation to protect the associate, the manager, and the company. We discuss how to maintain the associate's dignity and respect throughout the meeting and motivate them to do better next time. We finish the coaching with points on how to approach the situation. Once the meeting is complete, we look for feedback from the managers on how they felt things went and how it might be improved next time. It is a very collaborative process.

Other Management Coaching and Training Opportunities

Aside from the one-on-one involvement mentioned previously, we also offer classes that are currently taught internally. The purpose of these classes is to teach managers how to handle situations before they happen. One of our most utilized classes is titled Painless Performance Improvement. This four-hour session was developed specifically for our needs and is mandatory for all managers. During the past year, all store management and corporate executives have completed this training. Years of research has shown that organizations achieve greater performance from their associates when managers handle this process correctly, so we have resources for doing it right the first time!

Building a stronger team continues through additional training in the form of four leadership classes per year. The initial focus is on our frontline leaders. Once their training has been completed, the classes are available to the next level down until all managers and any high potential associates have been trained. Dale Carnegie's Human Relations class is available as well to all interested associates annually.

This year we have an organizational goal to provide mentoring as part of a strategic plan for improving our bench. Each leader throughout our company has been challenged with selecting a minimum of three individuals to mentor and develop. This initiative will increase going forward after we have all of the basics in place to teach this skill. To jump-start this initiative we rolled out a mentoring class for all of our leaders. It focuses on how to be a good mentor and provides some of the necessary tools for mentoring. This training includes a segment that teaches them that it can very often be a two-way street—mentoring helps develop the mentor as well as the mentee.

Although I do not know what precise training our local competitors offer, I believe some of what we do is very unique for our industry, especially for associates who are below the role of store manager. Not to say that we are the only ones to offer this type of training, but I believe that we are the only grocer in New England that provides training to impact our success plan.

Employee Talent Development

Our talent development and job training program began four years ago. The organization had fifteen individual, department specific, training modules that needed to be built from the ground up. As of today, eleven are completed. For example, we have manuals for our bakery, deli, produce, and other departments. These modules contain several sections to meet the training requirements of numerous positions per department. For example, a meat module covers training for a clerk, wrapper, cutter, assistant manager, and manager. How do you clean a slicer? What are the sanitation requirements? How do you prepare this food? How can we ensure that you are well trained and diverse in that department? All of these questions and many others are answered through the materials covered in their training module.

The employees have actually embraced these training options very well. We have received numerous positive comments and requests for additional materials. For many years, people were trained informally: someone came up and showed you how to do a good job. Between 2000 and 2007, the company basically doubled in size and a majority of those natural training opportunities were lost. Managers and associates no longer had as much time available for training as they were focused on assuring our customers had great service. Because of our increased size, many people now had several associates working beneath them, which made informal training more difficult. With this growth came the reality that our bench may require additional talent to maintain the strength that we had before. To address that, classes were created and continue to be added to the development process, enabling us to build in every area.

HR's Role in Providing the Moral Compass in Times of Change

Three of the most important skills that HR professionals need to effectively manage employee relations are patience, persuasiveness, and influence. People are not born leaders and HR professionals are not necessarily born HR professionals. However, they can learn to become negotiators and discover methods to get things accomplished with the least amount of resistance. Most companies look to their HR departments to be the leaders of change for the organization and to partner with other executives in how to make associates feel good about change and embrace it.

Being able to honestly communicate with everyone and being as transparent as possible helps achieve that. You can serve as the moral compass, so to speak, for the organization that seeks to do the right thing for everyone and exert a positive influence. People will believe that you are trying to find the best path to help everyone succeed, as opposed to advocating for one specific direction. This needs to be done across the company, which means involving your buyers, operations partners, accounting, marketing, and IT professionals, to name a few of our specific departments. Considering all of those people have to be engaged as well, you need to have that open dialogue with them and establish a comfort level so that they will feel they can come to you and trust that you will be able to help them. Sometimes it is a matter of being a conscience for others.

Face-to-face communication with employees is always the best scenario and we give our folks in the stores as much true face time as possible. The owners, executive management, directors, and HR representatives are in the stores several days a week. Traditional and cultural surveys are conducted to obtain feedback. This information gives us a better understanding of where we are doing well, what we may not be doing well, and how people feel about particular issues. These are completely anonymous surveys so that we may receive honest results. Proximity and comfort help create an open atmosphere and being out in the stores you hear things. People are quite at ease sharing in our organization to the point where, at times, they will actually call an owner as opposed to me or anyone in HR. For a company this size, that is amazing and very special.

Workplace Diversity, Inclusion, and Generational Differences

The best practices for managing diversity and inclusion in the workplace involve education and training. It is absolutely essential to ensure that all cultures are respected throughout the company, and to achieve that, we provide educational training classes for all associates. We also partner with our vendor community to increase our knowledge of specialty products that we sell. Our customers trust us to provide a wide variety of quality merchandise.

We also have many generations in our organization, which sometimes presents interesting challenges. Because our RSTO policy emphasizes respect for all, we try to offer something to everyone. The age range of our associates right now is fourteen to eighty-four. We have over two hundred fourteen to fifteen year olds and more than four hundred associates who are over the age of sixty with many of them exceeding seventy. Associates are allowed to do the type of work that they are physically capable of doing if they meet and maintain our minimum requirements. While some of the sixty- and seventy-year-olds in our check stands do not scan items as quickly as the fifteen- or sixteen-year-olds, they engage the customer. Consequently, they will have a line waiting for their check stand whereas there will not be a line waiting for the sixteen-year-old's check stand. So we coach the fourteen-, fifteen-, and sixteen-year-olds to engage the customer and encourage our sixty- and seventy-year-olds to remember that in addition to chatting with our customers, good service also includes getting them out the door a little bit quicker.

Maintaining a reasonable work-life balance also factors into our employee relations strategies. In Massachusetts, employers are required to pay time and a half on certain holidays and on Sundays. There have been times when full-time associates may become so interested in having the additional income that they might work too many hours. We strive to remind them to step back and remember that family is also important, even when money is tight. Another example of Roche Bros' family first philosophy is when the corporate office is notified that an associate has had a member of their family pass on, the company will send flowers or a meal to their home. The owners, managers, and other associates offer their personal condolences, thoughts, help, and prayers to the family. When you come to work for the Roche organization, you become part of the Roche extended family. Your family is now our family and our family is your family. We will do anything we can to help you take care of your family. We have an excellent employee assistance program with many extended benefits that are offered to everyone. I, personally, am proud and honored to be a part of Roche Bros.

Conclusion: Critical Advice for HR Professionals

In my opinion, a few of the biggest mistakes that HR professionals tend to make when they are managing employee relations is either sharing too much information, becoming personally involved, or not stepping back to review the situation before giving advice on a course of action. If you are not cautious, it is easy to say something that should not have been said or may be misunderstood. You should never commit to anything that you are unable to do because your reputation—and that of HR—is based on your word. Never make promises that you cannot fulfill.

The most important aspects of employee relations management that I would stress to an upcoming HR professional is strong communication, do not get personally involved, and always maintain clarity and resolution in everything that you do. Be certain that you represent the profession in a way that it is intended to be represented. Be confident.

Key Takeaways

- Show mutual respect to everyone—not just to the customers but also to each other. Try to live by the golden rule: always treat others as you would like to be treated.
- Most companies look to their HR departments to be the leaders of change for the organization and to partner with other executives in how to make associates feel good about change and embrace it.
- The top mistake that HR professionals tend to make when they are managing employee relations is either sharing too much information or becoming personally involved.
- Your reputation, and the success of HR, is based on your word. Never promise what you cannot deliver.

Jennie Fotovich is currently the vice president of human resources for Roche Bros. Supermarkets. Ms. Fotovich joined the Roche Bros. team in February of 2009. Roche Bros. is a family-owned company that has been in business in the Boston area for sixty years. The organization has approximately 4,400 associates with eighteen retail locations and a corporate headquarters located in Wellesley Hills, Massachusetts. As the senior HR officer, Ms. Fotovich is responsible for human resource initiatives including recruitment, leadership and associate development, training, compensation, benefits, compliance, and risk management.

Prior to relocating to New England, Ms. Fotovich worked in Texas with Minyard Food Stores and their other two banners, Carnival and Sack N Save. Her position as vice president of human resources and training encompassed many areas including staffing and training models for new store openings, succession planning, and compliance for sixty-five retail locations in the Dallas – Fort Worth area.

Before heading to Texas, Ms. Fotovich made a major move from working with McLane grocery distribution in Colorado to Florida to work with a very large grocer that was experiencing tremendous change. When she joined the human resource team in 2004, Winn Dixie had over 1,000 retail stores and more than 75,000 associates. After spending six months transitioning one of the manufacturing sites to new ownership, Ms.

Fotovich was promoted to regional human resource manager of more than 243 stores with approximately 19,000 associates. During the next eighteen months, she worked with a strategic team transitioning the footprint of the company through a dramatic downsizing as part of the company's reorganization strategy.

Ms. Fotovich is a member of SHRM, NEHRA (New England Human Resource Association), and a corporate member of the Network of Executive Women – New England.

Dedication: *This chapter is dedicated to my husband Steve who has always had faith in me and was there beside me through all of life's challenges. His never-ending support and encouragement helped me become the person I am and achieve my goals.*

Partnering with Leadership to Manage Employee Morale and Productivity in a Global, Complex, and Innovative Cultural Environment

Trina Maynes

Senior Vice President, Human Resources

Nickelodeon, a Viacom company

ASPATORE

Introduction

Currently, I serve as the senior vice president of human resources for Nickelodeon, a Viacom company. For the past sixteen years, I have had the opportunity to work in dynamic and complex organizations that place high value propositions on culture. In my role, I drive human resource strategy for the East Coast operations of Nickelodeon Network—a premier children's media outlet.

Human resources in a creative environment is a multi-faceted, complex function that is responsible for many lofty agendas, including curating the culture and instilling that sound employee relations principles are upheld. In this chapter, we will review some of the tenants that are needed to be considered when managing an employee relations function. Cultivating innovation, engaging leadership, diversity, talent development, and morale will be discussed.

Addressing Challenges Associated with Cultivating Innovation across the Organization

Innovation is the air in the body of creativity. In order for businesses who drive content to stay relevant there is an incessant need to innovate, redefine, and re-engage in a market that is ever evolving and changing. Being the best in any category is only as good as your last output.

Human resources is one vehicle within an organization that helps cultivate innovation in times of plenty and times of want. Both environments present opportunity to infuse strategic employee relations skills. In times of plenty, you are your biggest competitor. How do you raise the bar to heights higher than your last success? Whatever measure of success you experience—increased revenue, profound viewer ratings, or record-setting sales—the time for basking in your accomplishment can often be short lived.

Innovation in times of want looks and feels different. In times of want and complexity, the drive to innovation is often underpinned by uncertainty and fear. You are no longer competing against yourself, but rather an external force that has taken your share of the marketplace.

Addressing challenges associated with innovation require a surgical and intentional approach for leaders to manage the organization. Key fundamental practices are:

- Creating a vision (game plan) for where we need to be as a business
- Being clear about expectations
- Fostering an environment where ideation and risk is encouraged
- Communicating across all levels of the organization
- Listening to what is important to your stakeholders/employees
- Remaining optimistic while being authentic

A leader's role in days of uncertainty is to take hold of those tenants of innovation that made you famous. Human resources helps this happen by having a strong presence and developing change management tools that build and support new ways of thinking.

Engaging Leadership in the Responsibility for Managing Employee Relations

The responsibility for developing and maintaining employee relations is shared across the organization.

Human resource professionals play an integral role in providing sound advice, both legal and practical. Leaders, however, play a fundamental role in ensuring that organizational expectations are prophesized to the masses and demonstrated by their own actions.

Preparing managers to effectively implement strategies by talking about them, and demonstrating them on a daily basis, is critical. This is about walking the walk and talking the talk. It is on a daily basis that leaders get an opportunity to demonstrate those behaviors, which are needed to get great results from their people. Employees will quickly dismiss company policy to rhetoric when those behaviors are not upheld when the conference room door is closed.

Essential Skills for Managing Employee Relations

In order to manage employee relations effectively, leaders need to be equipped with a tool chest of skills. One of the more valuable skills needed to deliver sound employee relations is knowledge of labor and employment laws and regulations. A fundamental knowledge of how unfair employment practices affect the workplace is critical to any principle in an organization.

Employee relations is a discipline that requires an understanding of how business and sociological concepts come together to hurt working relationships. Sound analytical and critical-thinking skills are crucial to be able to identify potential threats and resolve them before they have a negative impact on the organization

A strong driver of employee relations is to be able to gather facts to access a situation, and synthesis the information down to be able to influence and coach employees to either stop or start a given set of actions. This ability to be able to influence and communicate is necessary to be an effective change agent in an organization.

What sabotages healthy employee relations is subjectivity, emotion, inconsistency, and a lack of transparency.

Best Practices for Managing Diversity and Inclusion in the Workplace

The ability to effectively manage a diverse workforce is essential for all global organizations. As the cultural footprint within companies continues to grow and expand beyond our borders, it is necessary for organizations to embrace inclusivity.

Inclusion underscores that each individual brings a unique set of experiences, preconceived notions, thought processes, and work styles with them when they walk through the door each day. The way in which an organization chooses to manage those differences speaks to their diversity practices.

In focusing on the purest concept of diversity, it involves creating an environment where an individual is able to come into the workplace to professionally bring their whole self to the organization without fear of reprisal or punishment.

Organizations that manage diversity properly have found ways in which to value the unique talents of their employees while ensuring that all employees have the ability to be able to succeed.

For those organizations that have embraced diversity, it entails ensuring that everyone has a voice and has a purpose. Inclusions can look and feel differently across various workforces. Those organizations that manage diversity well have provided platforms for broad constituents to be able to share ideas, discuss what is meaningful, and to drive creative solutions to everyday business challenges that surface.

Talent Development and Career Training

In today's work environment, managing and growing your career is your responsibility.

Human resources can be fundamental to helping employees through the self-exploration process that is needed to grow one's career. The evolution of navigating your career involves a fluid set of steps that work toward helping the employee articulate their talent, build their personal brand, and create an action plan. The steps to talent growth include:

- Knowing your strengths, weaknesses, and areas of talent
- Having a clear point of view of where they want to be
- Creating a plan to get there
- Committing to the plan and building a support group of champions and advocates

Organizations are beginning to see the return in the investment in helping guide their employees through this cycle.

Monitoring Employee Morale

Monitoring employee morale requires that HR professionals and organizational leaders have a presence and connection to their employees. When employees are happy they perform their jobs more efficiently, which improves the success of any business.

The core of a leader's role is to find a way to capture the hearts and the minds of their teams. How effective you are at accomplishing this can be measured using various methods from informal private conversations to assessing data with climate surveys or exit interviews.

Strong HR partnership allows for employees to have a safe, trusting environment to discuss the corporate culture. If a trusted environment has been created, employees will have a sense of comfort in sharing what is working well in the organization and what red flags should be given attention.

Strong organizations that have leaders who are attuned to the well-being of their organization can also be a fundamental tool in monitoring morale. An executive who is able to assess how we are doing, not how I want us to be doing, is skilled in their ability to read their people and to understand their needs.

The strongest gauge in evaluating employee morale is to look at data. Exit surveys that detail why an employee has made a decision to leave an organization will point to trends and patterns that should be paid attention to. This confidential tool will unearth meaningful information that can inform areas that require improvement.

Evolving New Employee Relations Management Strategies to Maintain Alignment with Business Objectives

Sound employee relations strategies need to be grounded in business objectives to be relevant to your organization.

To be affective in promoting employee productivity, an intentional and concerted set of actions needs to be driven by human resources and an organization's leadership.

Managing the employee relations for an organization is fundamentally about managing culture. It is a very important objective for anyone that is looking to get into this field, and involves keeping your finger on the pulse of the organization and knowing what is an important goal we are working toward as a business, and the agreement that we make about how we will engage each other along the way.

Conclusion

As companies become more complex and corporate stakes continue to grow, the importance of solid employee relations practices has become more essential.

Human resource organizations have traditionally owned employee relations as a function of their role to promote strong organizations. However, as the stakes for all businesses increase, it is clear that all leaders need to be good stewards of smart employee relations practices.

The role of the effective employee relations leader will emerge as a critical stakeholder, whose role is to influence strong employer and employee relationships. The successful leader will be able to create trusting environments where policies underscore values and allow for excellent work.

Our ability to remain competitive in this global marketplace requires that we find ways to mine for innovation, be intentional about how we shape our cultural environments, and engage the workforce in bringing consistent and excellent work.

Key Takeaways

- An organization that promotes healthy employee relations practices sets culture as a priority. High value propositions are placed on creating environments where employees bring their best talents and innovation to the office each day.
- The most perceptive organizations ensure that sound employee relations principles are aligned to overall business objectives by underscoring how we agree to engage each other while we work toward our goals.
- To be effective as a steward of employee relations, leaders need to communicate their expectations and hold the organizations accountable to living up to their standards.

Trina Maynes is senior vice president of human resources for Nickelodeon's East Coast Television, Digital, Consumer Products, Recreation and Original Movies businesses, including Nick Jr, TeenNick, and Nicktoons. In this role, Ms. Maynes is responsible for developing the strategic human resource direction of Nickelodeon through partnership with EVP, Human Resources.

Under Ms. Maynes' leadership, a team of human resource professionals are responsible for helping Nickelodeon retain its competitive edge through organizational effectiveness and operational excellence.

Ms. Maynes' background includes more than fifteen years of human resources experience. She joined Viacom/MTV Networks in 1996 and has progressed through the organization in progressively advanced positions. Before her current role, she managed all human resource functions for Vh1, LOGO, and Harmonix Games. Prior to coming to MTV Networks, she was an employee relations manager at Calvin Klein. She began her career at Simon & Schuster where she worked for five years as a human resource generalist.

Ms. Maynes holds a master's of education degree in counseling psychology from Columbia University and a bachelor of science from Fordham University.

Dedication: This piece is dedicated to those leaders, colleagues, mentors, employees, and champions who have provided experiences and moments to grow and contribute.

Maximizing Employee Engagement from Point of Hire

Keith A. Chrzanowski
Senior Vice President, Global Human Resources
Given Imaging

ASPATORE

Introduction

Since pioneering the field of capsule endoscopy in 2001, Given Imaging has become a world leader in GI medical devices, offering health care providers a range of innovative options for visualizing, diagnosing, and monitoring the digestive system. The company offers a broad product portfolio including PillCam® video capsules for the small bowel, esophagus, and colon (PillCam® COLON not approved for use in the United States), industry-leading ManoScan™ high-resolution manometry, and Bravo® pH and Digitrapper® pH and impedance monitoring. Given Imaging is committed to delivering breakthrough innovations to the GI community and supporting its ongoing clinical needs. Given Imaging's headquarters are located in Yoqneam, Israel, with operating subsidiaries in the United States, Germany, France, Japan, Australia, Vietnam, and Hong Kong. Today we have more than 780 employees worldwide.

In my role as the senior vice president of HR, we are committed to building a competitive advantage for Given Imaging through the quality, capability, and performance of our people. We have key HR leadership in Israel, Europe, Asia, and the United State. We work to enable the growth and financial performance of Given Imaging by ensuring we have a solid foundation of understanding related to the business (financial performance, products, and strategic plan), deliver excellence in HR functional responsibilities, and foster a high-performing culture. Employee relations fit within our goal of creating and maintaining a high-performance culture.

Defining Employee Relations Management

While there can be many components to creating a high-performance culture, we particularly value:

- Talent acquisition
- Leadership development and succession planning
- Change management
- Employee relations

Our approach to employee relations is part of our approach to creating a high-performance culture. Employee relations management is comprised of many different compliance related activities, as well as activities that highlight the organizational values of an organization. These values provide a framework for decision making and interaction, so it is important that employees share them.

Managing Employee Relations from the Point of Hire

Most employers today are effective in offering to employees basic components of an employee relations program, though they/we may not label them as "The Employee Relations Program."

So what are the basics? HR, whether through an employment contract (required in many foreign countries and unionized operations) or offer of employment, sends the first message as to the employee's place in the company's hierarchy. We need to ensure this interaction is professional and focused on the employee's knowledge acquisition as they embark with their new organization.

Next, the post-recruitment process should be well planned, with on-boarding and assimilation to provide the employee an understanding of not only "what" they must do to be successful but also "how" they must work to be successful. At Given Imaging, each employee must complete an online orientation that covers:

- Video introduction from our CEO Homi Shamir
- Company history
- Products/disease statistics
- Code of business conduct
- Employee handbook
- Whistleblower policy
- Health care compliance

Following this online on-boarding, a schedule of introductory meetings takes place to ensure the new employee meets and understands those individuals in the organization who are important to his or her job activities.

Additionally, the employee lifecycle process (see diagram) is shared with the employee so that they may further understand the competencies and expectations of Given Imaging.

**Given Imaging
Annual Employee Lifecycle**

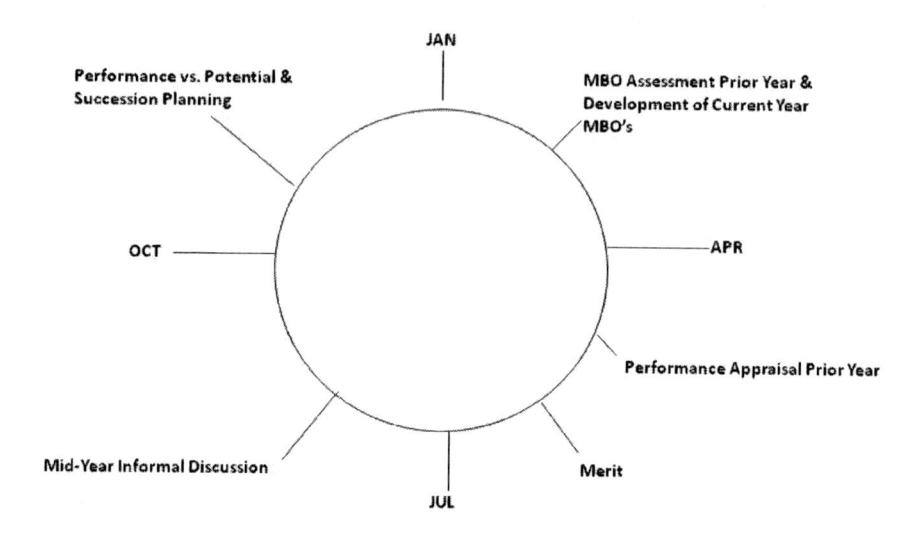

- JAN: (top)
- Performance vs. Potential & Succession Planning
- MBO Assessment Prior Year & Development of Current Year MBO's
- OCT
- APR
- Performance Appraisal Prior Year
- Mid-Year Informal Discussion
- Merit
- JUL

Our belief is that if employee engagement is maximized early, the employee will more quickly and fully contribute to the organization and to overall performance.

The Most Important Skills for Managing Employee Relations

HR is responsible for effectively maintaining an environment that prevents and resolves problems involving employees that arise from or could affect performance. The HR professional must be seen by management and employees as someone who:

- Knows the business
- Works to match business needs with employee profiles
- Understands the future of the business
- Fosters open communication

- Knows the employees and has fact-based opinions on their strengths and development needs

If the HR professional can master these skills, he or she will be viewed in the right way and will be well positioned to act in a balanced manner toward mediation and conflict resolution that may impact overall organizational performance. The key is to be seen as the employee advocate while representing management. To strike this balance, it is important to focus on the many other possible components of an effective employee relations strategy, including communication, consistency, and change management.

Best Practices for Communicating Effectively Around Employee Relations Issues

Building on the theme of a proactive employee relations strategy, there are several other components that should be included to ensure that potential issues are identified early. Communication activities between employees and management are key to this effort. This should happen under the assumption that employees and management alike desire success for the organization. It is important to provide forums to give employees a chance to be heard, and to let them understand the performance of the business and their contribution to its successes.

Our annual employee lifecycle serves to align performance and development and is a foundational communication activity. Additionally, following the release of the financial results each quarter, a "Letter from the CEO" is sent via e-mail to all employees. This covers financial performance, key achievements, and direction for the organization as we move forward. These "Letters from the CEO" serve to make Given Imaging visible as a global entity and connect employees and management alike to our successes and challenges.

After each quarter, the CEO and select senior managers host a meeting to review the previous quarter in terms of financial performance, key achievements, and patients' stories that serve to demonstrate the impact we are having on lives. Employees are recognized during these meetings, and if appropriate, we share their stories. Employee questions are encouraged as an opportunity to further drive the sharing of information. We are a global organization, so cultural norms do tend to drive employee participation in asking questions.

The third component in our communication activity is the semiannual employee newsletter. Again we focus on key achievements, shows, and community service features. Most importantly, we weave in patient stories that help all employees to connect with the impact their efforts have on people's lives.

Closing the Feedback Loop

The "Letter from the CEO," quarterly employee meetings, and our newsletter serve to provide access and information, and ensure that employees are in synch with the organization. It is also important to our employee relations strategy that employees are heard. While there is some opportunity for this in the employee meeting, we use other formal and informal methods.

While most are familiar with the old adage of "managing by walking around," in a global organization with many field-based employees this may not always be possible. We encourage management to communicate on a regular basis with both their direct reports and levels below through regular one-on-one calls and during meetings. This is a key part of identifying possible conflicts occurring in the organization. HR must have the confidence of management and work with them to resolve issues that arise.

More formally, Given Imaging maintains an "open door" policy that allows any employee at any time to approach management (most often HR) with concerns and questions. Interestingly, 75 percent of these interactions are not interpersonal conflict but center on process collaboration and efficiency. Whether the conflict, question, or concern is process related or more personal, HR serves to work with the employee and other employees or managers to mediate and resolve the issue.

Follow-Up and Resolution

Timeliness of follow-up and resolution is key and must be a top priority for the HR professional. When an employee has taken the step of reaching out to others in an organization, it is fair to say that for them the issue is of great importance. In some ways, employees view timeliness of follow-up through the lens of their value to the organization. The organization sends a clear message to the employee through prompt follow-up and setting expectations for a possible resolution that the employee is valued.

There are many other methods to ensure that employees are heard and involved in a next-steps plan. One effective method is the "jump-level meeting." This is a powerful way for leaders to have highly effective conversations with employees. The term "jump-level" applies when a manager skips over his direct report(s) to meet one-on-one with their direct reports. The meeting may last thirty to forty-five minutes and is focused on a clearly defined set of questions to inventory alignment on:

- Clear and elevating goals
- Results driven structure
- Process efficiency/accelerated decision making
- Collaborative climate
- Understanding standards of excellence
- Recognition
- Leadership/commitment

Following completion of the meeting(s), the leader and HR meet to discuss the summary and action plan. The leader then feeds back to each participant(s) the roll-up feedback/action plan, and ensures that when appropriate the employee is a part of the resolution or contributes to the action plan.

The wins for management are: unfiltered bottoms-up feedback; validation of issues/opportunities; development and enhancement of employee trust and confidence in the organization; and increased employee satisfaction as change occurs. The wins for the employee: increased insight and awareness of business strategies/initiatives; understanding and learning from the top-down; and an opportunity to discuss and get clarification on the big-picture view of roles and expectations.

Keeping a Figure on the Pulse of Employee Morale

How does the HR professional know the positive or negative impact of the organization's efforts on employee morale and culture? Throughout my HR career, I have found that metrics are an important part of monitoring the success or failure of an organization's efforts related to employee relations and creating a high-performance culture.

We maintain a dashboard of metrics that enable us to maintain focus on our efforts. We do not call these HR metrics but rather management metrics. Our purpose is to obligate all managers to understand the role they play in employee relations and the creation of a high-performance culture.

Metrics that are important indicators of an organization's success or failure include:

- Talent acquisition – Time-to-fill and cost-per-hire can give viability to the performance of recruitment process management.
- Turnover (voluntary and involuntary) – We want to know why employees are leaving (exit interviews) and how effectively managers are addressing underperformance.
- Training and development – Cost per employee and training hours per employee help us to see if we are investing in the growth and development of our workforce as we commit to do in the annual employee lifecycle.
- Diversity of our workforce – Do we accurately reflect the country, region, and customer profile in which we operate?

These metrics are presented to senior management on a monthly basis and trends and action plans are identified and discussed.

The Most Important Aspects of Employee Relations Management

Employee relations management is not a stand-alone set of activities that ensure "good" employee relations; employee relations is a component of creating and fostering organizational success.

MAXIMIZING EMPLOYEE ENGAGEMENT FROM POINT OF HIRE

The process of fostering success starts when an individual joins the organization (on-boarding and assimilation) and must have many touch points each year, whether formal:

- Annual employee lifecycle communication
  - Management by objectives (MBOs)
  - Performance appraisal
  - Mid-year performance discussion
  - Talent review/development
- Letter from the CEO
- Quarterly meetings
- Employee newsletter
- Open door policy
- Jump-level meetings

Or informal:

- Management via walking or talking around

Conclusion

To develop credibility with the management team, HR must know the business and deliver HR functional excellence through process design and ownership of recruitment, employee welfare, compensation management, change management, training, and leadership development. It is also important to match business needs with employee profiles, foster open communication, and know the employees and have fact-based opinions on their strengths and development needs. The employees must view HR as a highly approachable advocate that takes a balanced approach to mediating and resolving questions, concerns, or conflict. The same characteristics that are critical to gaining management credibility also contribute greatly to how HR is viewed by all other employees.

When an HR professional can effectively strike the balance between employee advocate and management representative, he or she will be well positioned to drive the employee relations strategy of a company.

Key Takeaways

- Employee relations management fits within the goal of creating and maintaining a high-performance culture.
- Organizational values provide a framework for decision making and interaction, so it is important that employees share them.
- If employee engagement is maximized early, the employee will more quickly and fully contribute to the organization and to overall performance.
- When an employee has identified an issue, it is HR's responsibility to follow up promptly and thoroughly. This sends a clear message to the employee about his or her value to the organization.

Keith A. Chrzanowski has served as Given Imaging's senior vice president of human resources since January 1, 2008. Prior to that, from January 2005 until December 2007, he was the director of human resources of the Americas region. Prior to joining Given Imaging, from July 2002 until January 2005 Mr. Chrzanowski was senior director/vice president of human resources for McKesson Provider Technologies, a division of McKesson specializing in delivering software to include automation and robotics, business process reengineering, analytics, and other services that connect health care providers, physicians, payors, and patients across all care settings. From July 2000 until July 2002 Mr. Chrzanowski was vice president of human resources for Spherion's Outsourcing Group, which provided services to Fortune 500 customers. From 1991 to 2000, Mr. Chrzanowski worked as a human resource manager and director of human resources for diagnostic and medical supply divisions which initially were a part of Baxter Healthcare and eventually acquired by Cardinal Health in 1999. Prior to joining Baxter, Mr. Chrzanowski worked for Schlumberger Industries in the United States and Canada as a human resources manager from 1987 until 1991. From 1983 until 1987, Mr. Chrzanowski held a variety of human resources positions in support of Beecham's Consumer Products businesses. Mr. Chrzanowski has a BA in communications from Western Illinois University and an MA in organizational theory from Norwich University.

Strategic Business Drivers for High-Performing People Practices

Brenda Rogers
Vice President, Human Resources
Roku Inc.

ASPATORE

Introduction

As the vice president of human resources at a late stage start up, I have a small team. My role at Roku is primarily focused on growth, finding the best talent, and building the organization capability to develop and deliver the game changing products. We have built a strong staffing function to support the hyper-growth over the last fourteen months. My team is also responsible for putting systems and processes in that we need to support our internal customers. Our managers are ultimately responsible for their own hiring and retention of top talent, as we provide the tools, data, and expertise to ensure their success.

We are a culture of self-responsibility with senior-level people in all areas. Our organization aims to hire the highly regarded and talented people who have an average of over twenty years of experience with very few junior positions. We usually hire senior people that are hands-on and tactical as well as strategic so they can take the organization to the next level, anticipating future needs. As a result, leadership development and training at Roku is atypical for most organizations of our size and stage. I take seriously my responsible for ensuring that our high-performing culture is maintained and is considered in all decisions affecting people, processes, and the environment. It is not necessarily about driving the culture, but more about understanding, maintaining, and being respectful of the culture that has been an important part of our success from the beginning.

Maintaining Culture

While our culture, like most companies, originated from a visionary founding CEO, I help maintain it by being involved in many of the strategic decisions within the organization. It is not only the strategic decisions that can affect culture, but also the small things that cross all organizations. Not everybody is thinking about the effects of their decisions from that perspective. I use a lens when making decisions, looking at what we do and how we do it. My lens takes into consideration the way we communicate, make decisions, organize, and recognize and reward people. We are not an overly process-oriented organization, and avoid anything that looks like red tape and politics. If a process gets in the way of getting work done and does not add value, we do not do it. We do what makes sense and people feel empowered and are expected to make great decisions without permission. It can be pretty dynamic with all of these factors at play.

Employee Relations Management

Employee relations are something that we do not talk about formally or in traditional ways. I would define my role as more of a coaching and problem-solving role. But there are very few issues at Roku that I would categorize as employee relations, as the culture of self-responsibility fosters individuals resolving their own problems directly. It is something that everybody at Roku does. Ultimately, it comes down to employees managing their own issues and taking responsibility for their concerns or problems. Many of the typical employee relations issues do not require a great deal of HR involvement because the organization and the individuals are responsible, so HR's role is more like a coach and advisor to the employees when issues arise.

FIGURE 1: LEVERAGING TUCKMAN'S MODEL FOR TEAM DYNAMICS

Forming, Storming, Norming, Performing...

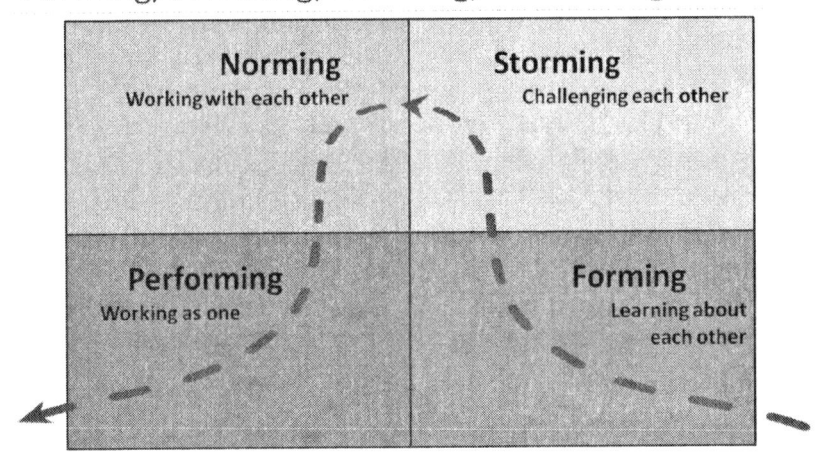

Norming	Storming
Working with each other	Challenging each other
Performing	**Forming**
Working as one	Learning about each other

Most common issues are mostly around growth right now. We are a private company that is growing at a phenomenal rate with an increase in revenue, product, and people. We have more than doubled revenue, tripled product sales, and doubled our employee population, all within a one-year period.

Rapid growth usually leads to change, and change usually provokes discomfort in most people. In our case, we hire individuals who thrive in changing environments and are flexible, nimble, do not require much direction, and know how to figure out what needs to get done. With growth comes the rapid addition to existing teams and the formation of new teams. Theories such as Tuckman's model for team dynamics provide a lens for ensuring teams can be their most productive (see figure 1).

Developing Employee Relations Strategies

I meet with the managers and executives regularly to discuss strategies and issues related to their employees and teams. While most issues are around hiring and building teams, we discuss and develop strategies to accomplish program and project goals and then how we will actually get them done and with whom. Identifying the right skills and talent required is a key to good decisions. A great deal of decision making starts with high-level planning and then evolves into a more detailed tactical plan. So I guess you could say I get involved in the business planning stage involving talent. A technique I use often is asking the questions that allow the technical expert to reflect and examine all possible solutions. Some solutions are identified that may not have been uncovered without asking those necessary questions. Providing what-if scenarios, evaluating risk-benefit outcomes, and providing a sounding board to decision makers, we work together to develop strategies for organizational change. I find it to be effective to start by asking questions about the expectations for the ultimate goal and then ask more questions about how something can get done or how it will play out. I find it easy to drive people to problem solve as a team by just asking the right questions. I see myself as an enabler rather than the stereotypical HR policy police.

The Importance of Communication

We prepare our managers for situations through constant communication. I think developing solid working relationships is all about having honest conversations and putting things on the table. I can bring an unbiased perspective and remove emotion from decisions. We do a great deal of hallway conversations, and that is easier in the open cube environment. This leads to many open conversations that occur every day, and overall it is a very honest environment with no politics to get in the way. We do not have structured management training or rules that constrain how to get things done. We do have some philosophies that we share and expect everyone to do the right thing. Communicating those expectations early in the interview process, during the on-boarding process, and in regular one-on-one and team meetings reinforces and promotes the expected results. We move at a very fast pace, so communication is important to keep everyone informed and aware of any changes and aligned with each individual's priorities. Keeping each other informed is an important value and can become difficult if it is not a priority during rapid growth. I believe a great deal of dysfunction can stem from miscommunication, and if everyone is participating in collaborative conversations and making sure that the right people are involved in those discussions, it results in high-performing organizations like Roku.

FIGURE 2: PRINCIPLES FOR COMMUNICATING EFFECTIVELY

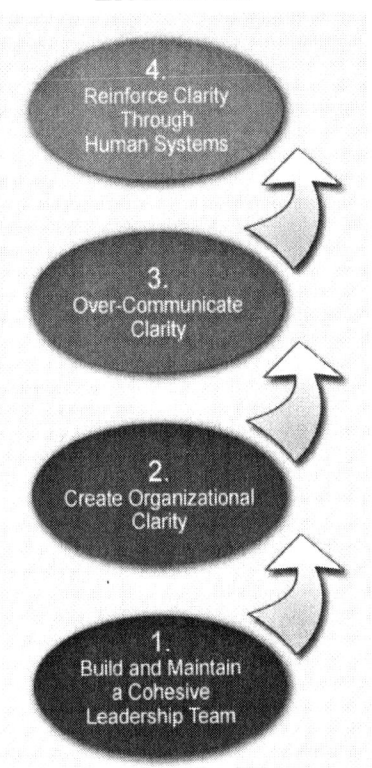

4. Reinforce Clarity Through Human Systems
3. Over-Communicate Clarity
2. Create Organizational Clarity
1. Build and Maintain a Cohesive Leadership Team

Patrick Lencioni identified the importance of communication in *The Four Obsessions of an Extraordinary Executive*. These principles are alive at Roku (see figure 2).

Important HR Skills

After understanding the business, I think good judgment, an understanding of organizational culture, and a strong sense of human behavior are all important HR skills. There are some factors and pitfalls that you cannot necessarily learn from a course or degree. And many HR professionals have learned on the job through mentors and strong leaders. Important skills and techniques can also be learned though research, reading, and networking with peers. But not everyone is cut out for an HR role. I have survived and succeeded in companies with very different types of cultures. The most satisfying experiences are more likely when the company and your own values are aligned. The kinds of things that I experienced while working for a large global company are different from the kinds of employee relations problems present at a small private company. People are people though, so the potential for having similar problems exists. I think that HR professionals prepare by having a solid business background, a respect for organizational culture, strong communication skills, and excellent problem-solving skills.

Understanding Human Behavior

An understanding of human behavior can be developed to some degree, but I think not everybody is equipped to deal with the social sciences. I know colleagues who love employee relations because they like helping people—your stereotype of an HR professional. But a simple employee relations issue can quickly turn into something serious like a sexual harassment investigation or dangerous like potential violence in the workplace. Studies have shown there are skills and abilities that are innate in individuals. Those skills equip them to deal with human behavior issues better than others. For example, I would not put your typical software engineer who is brilliant at writing code and likes solitude to develop that code in an employee relations position. This is an example of those who are left brain versus right brain. This theory of the structure and functions of the mind suggests that the two different sides of the brain control two different "modes" of thinking. It also suggests that each of us prefers one mode over the other. Understanding human behavior does require people skills and being self-aware. While we all have innate tendencies, I think that there is a great deal that you can learn by just being curious, taking courses, reading, or working with those you respect who have experiences they are willing to share with you.

Maintaining Communication

At the highest level, organizations can communicate with regular all-hands meetings. This is where we gather every employee in the company and provide strategic information. Formats vary and frequency can evolve from more often to less often as a company grows. In global companies, consideration for logistics, remote employees, time zones, topics, who speaks/presents, and length are important details. HR can have a role in ensuring all of these factors are considered through the culture lens. Topics should include what information is necessary and helpful for the majority of the employees. Information common in this format includes the status of technical projects, products, sharing of competitive data, the financials, and organization changes. All-hands can be difficult to maintain as companies grow from small to medium. Having these regular meetings is something that we do well, but know it will become challenging as the company grows. We are still able to continue regular meetings, but in planning for the future my role is to ensure we can keep communications a priority as we scale to global markets, exploring technologies that enable the sharing of information.

There is a great deal of information that we at Roku share with employees through company-wide e-mail updates as well. Some larger organizations have intranet systems to provide a sort of internal homepage of information on employee's computer systems. This is a modern platform for the traditional version of the company newsletter.

Managing a Diverse, Multi-Generational Workforce

Some of our best practices for managing diversity and inclusion start in the hiring process, where we look for specific skills, experience, and expertise. The result in focusing on the required skills invariably includes diverse types of people.

Our workforce is mostly made up of very experienced and seasoned professionals, and therefore it is predominantly baby boomers. We do have a multi-generational workforce, but not evenly across generations. Recognizing the generational differences between GenX (born between the early 1960s through the 1970s), GenY (born between the late 1970s to early 1980s), and baby boomers (born between 1946 and 1964) is helpful in understanding what motivates each and every employee. Research has provided data supporting that different generations are motivated by different things. Generations also communicate in different ways whether it is through social networks, telephone, e-mail, or traditional conversations. We plan for company events and meetings that involve everybody and therefore take those generational differences into account. We try to be aware of how people communicate, how they want to be informed, and what they are interested in doing.

By learning the motivations and generational footprint of each segment, we can leverage our talents and capitalize on the diversity of our teams. But rather than make assumptions by generation alone, we actually ask each employee what motivates them. No matter what the generation, we respect each other's values and differences and focus on the company goals and how each individual can contribute to our collective success. We manage expectations through open communication and goal clarity.

Work-Life Balance

Our company's work-life balance is healthy and we have what we call a high work-life balance satisfaction factor. People at Roku do not expect to be micromanaged. The business is managed and people are individually responsible. An example is our PTO non-policy where everyone is able to take as much time off as they want, as long as the work gets done. No accrual, no waiting periods, no request forms, no red tape. People plan responsibly and communicate with their managers, keeping everyone informed. We really do not know how much time people take off because we do not track it, but we know everyone takes vacations and are very satisfied with the freedom this provides. It requires a culture of trust for this to work and at Roku it works well. It is demonstrated from the top down.

Our culture is innovative at its core and we value a positive attitude. We also have a clear expectation of self-responsibility with a culture of self-discipline and freedom. Instead of having a culture of process that can get in the way of progress, we have found that by hiring senior people and allowing them to do what they do best, we create this amazing culture. Our culture enables us to create products faster, with innovating technology ultimately providing more value for our customers. Our competitors just cannot do that.

Flexible Scheduling

When people come to work and when they leave is irrelevant to us—our schedules are flexible. The fact that they get the job done is what is important. In this day of 24/7 connectivity, it is not realistic to think that a workday can be confined between the hours of 9 to 5. We work a very compact workday and our employees go home for dinner at a reasonable time. We have showers on site that employees appreciate when working out at lunch. Some employees run together, others have a regular soccer game at the park in the neighborhood, and quite a few ride their bikes to work. It is a very nice environment, even without a fancy gym.

Conclusion

In summary, fostering a positive work environment has many benefits. A true HR leader with a focus on the business can help to create that positive environment. When people are trusted to do their best and communication is abundant then satisfaction is high, engagement is high, and productivity is high. High-performing organizations are a direct result of these organizational attributes. Businesses are successful when organizations are high performing. Employees win, customers win, investors win. A visionary leader who sets the high bar knows how to hire the best, and values what a strong HR leader can contribute and lets them do what they do best. Roku is a real example of organizational excellence in every way and is an exciting place to have an impact.

Key Takeaways

- HR employees are most successful when they act as enablers rather than police. Motivating people to problem solve is simple if you ask the right questions.
- Managing various generations requires an understanding of what motivates each group and individuals to ensure everyone feels understood and appreciated.
- Allowing employees unlimited vacation time fosters an environment of trust and greatly impacts the company culture and the overall morale in the workplace.
- Innovation can flourish when process does not get in the way of progress.

Brenda Rogers is the vice president of human resources at Roku, the leading Internet streaming platform that is changing the television industry. It is a cool company in hyper growth mode, every HR leader's dream. As an expert at leading critical business initiatives through talent acquisition, organizational development, and workforce planning, Ms. Rogers is known for her keen business acumen. Companies where human capital is a key strategic advantage require this kind of HR leader.

Ms. Rogers previously served as vice president of human resources at Perlegen Sciences, the early genomics pioneer. After its sale to Genetic Technologies in 2010, Ms. Rogers consulted in high-growth VC backed organizations, such as QuantaLife, Relypsa, Ingenuity Systems, and previously Genomic Health. Prior to Genomic Health, Ms. Rogers was the vice president of human resources at the Institute for OneWorld Health, and held HR leadership roles at the San Jose State University Research Foundation, Portal Software (now Oracle), and Seagate Technology.

Ms. Rogers received professional human resources certification through the Society for Human Resources Management, completed University of Michigan's HR Executive Program under Dave Ulrich, and holds a bachelor's degree in communications from University of California, Santa Cruz. She is also a graduate of Leadership San Francisco, class of 2008. Ms. Rogers is also serving as board past president and membership VP for the Bay Area Human Resource Executives Council and on the advisory boards of Gallop Ventures and Raynak Executive Search.

Dedication: *I would like to dedicate this chapter to the forward thinking HR professionals who are business people first, with courage to break the rules and give the HR profession a better name. A few of them who have influenced my thinking are Patty McCord, CHO at Netflix, Deborah Barber, executive and organizational consultant, and Aryae Coopersmith, founder and CEO, HR Forums.*

Effective Global HR and Business Leadership

Barry Hartunian
*Chief Talent Officer and
Vice President, Human Resources*
Communispace

ASPATORE

Introduction

As chief talent officer and vice president of human resources for Communispace, I am responsible for constantly innovating and improving the employee experience for our fast-moving and fast-growing organization. Communispace builds, manages, and facilitates online communities for Fortune 100 Companies, for market research and customer engagement purposes. The range of expertise of our more than 400 employees includes client management, technology and engineering, sales and marketing, and research as well as product management.

While I am directly responsible for driving both our people strategy as well as day-to-day HR operations (talent acquisition, compensation, benefits, learning and development, employee relations, and business partnering functions), in my role I am also able to dedicate a significant portion of time to both leading and supporting our business as we grow rapidly across the globe.

Our highly collaborative employee culture is a result of true transparency; we strive to keep our employees knowledgeable and engaged in all that we do. Creativity plays a crucial role in that engagement and influences how employees do their work and interact with one another. It is this highly creative element that ultimately creates and sustains our culture on a daily basis, and impacts all levels of the organization—not only our executives and senior staff but every single employee no matter what organization they are in, where they reside in the world, or how long they have been here. We recognize that a fully engaged global staff promotes highly contributing employees who in turn provide best in class service to our clients. Our employee programs, communication channels, and work environment support this thriving culture of engagement and involvement.

Employee Programs

Through a variety of employee programs, we strive to positively support and develop our team members across the globe. Our Wellness Programs promote healthy activities like onsite yoga and exercise classes and e-coaching for mind and body wellness, as well as healthy meal delivery to name just a few. We encourage our employees to embrace those programs, which often compliment their lifestyles and interests.

Our Culture Committee has been intimately involved in business programs and decisions, as well as creating events and special occasions for our employees. This team, consisting of more than twenty-five employees across the organization, provides a unique perspective and is able to be a sounding board and, more accurately, are active contributors and decision makers in company programs.

Above and beyond our corporate contributions, our employees contribute personal time and energy toward dozens of charitable organizations every year. We are committed to providing everyone with time to participate and give back to their community. All our employees, worldwide, receive two days each year to use for any kind of volunteer activity that interests them. People can choose to use that time to work for an organization or cause that they are personally passionate about or participate in a larger group that is volunteering locally. For example, the HR team volunteered with the Rose Kennedy Greenway Conservancy (Boston). The Greenway encompasses gardens, plazas, and tree-lined promenades within the city of Boston. The Greenway is a key feature of the modern reinvention of Boston, Boston Harbor, and the South Boston Waterfront. We felt it was important to give back to the community where we work every day; doing something that was environmentally friendly was an added benefit.

Our Volunteer Committee, in which I play an advisory role, helps to identify and promote charitable opportunities for anyone who wants to get involved in this way. As an advisor, I highly value the opportunity to not only provide guidance when helpful, but also remain quite active in giving back to our local communities.

Recently, we piloted a program called "Dream Meetings" between employees and senior members of our leadership team. They are designed to be motivational as well as exploratory in nature—identifying areas in which the employee is passionate and how those passions might be leveraged in their current, or future, roles. The discussions are highly customized to the employee and topics range from career advancement in the short or long term as well as life and community involvement outside the office. As part of the process, the individual and executive discuss the employee's plan of action and next steps. These are then followed up with the employee sharing the ongoing progress they have made.

Communication Channels

People listen and learn through a variety of ways. We really feel very strongly about communicating to our staff in multiple methods. While some people prefer to share and learn through e-mail, others like in-person meetings, or all-staff meetings, and, being a global company, we often leverage technology through videoconferencing, conference calls, and voicemail.

Our company intranet was developed as a tool for all our employees to learn and engage. Affectionately referred to as "The Hub," we use it to disseminate a wide variety of information globally from new employee introductions and recent promotions to updates on our business and clients. We share information from all parts of the organization such as branding guidelines from marketing, inter-company project updates, HR program overviews, and announcing global initiatives. As the source for a host of current and relevant information, our intranet is used by employees on a daily basis.

In addition, every other week we have a global all-staff meeting. For sixty minutes, all our employees in Boston, New York, San Francisco, London, Shanghai, and Sydney dial in to hear the latest updates on the state of the business, new and exciting company initiatives, product roadmaps, and financial updates, as well as amazing and impactful work we have recently done for clients.

Another communication channel that is extremely effective is our CEO's weekly voicemail message, which goes out to all staff at the end of each week to highlight all different aspects of our business. The content might be about a specific impactful contribution one employee or a team has made, an update about the business, or an announcement of a new client or current market information.

Our senior management actively participates in weekly executive operation meetings where we evaluate and assess our financials, current and upcoming sales, client status and satisfaction, and HR and people initiatives and updates. All senior management is actively involved in annual financial and business planning for the company to ensure we are continuously aligned.

Leveraging Both Local and Global Perspectives in a Multinational Business Environment

With employees of all levels across the globe, many of our staff have strong connections to their local culture, and happily share their views based on those affiliations While employees who are based in other countries may benefit, at times, leveraging and learning from what has been successful in the United States (or any other country that is different from their own), this does not mean that one size fits all. When dealing with employees outside of the headquarters' home country, many tend to be unaware of regional and cultural differences. They may unknowingly try to force fit a solution that has been successful for them elsewhere. When working with a global workforce, listening is critical. You do not want to jump to headquarters-centric views and/or solutions, as many do.

Typically, when we open an operation outside of the United States, we hire local team members and complement that team with individuals who have worked with us for several years from another office. This makes for a great combination that helps fuel our global expansions: the longer-term employees know our business, while local employees know the particular regional culture and norms as well as how best to access local resources to start and grow the business.

Earlier in my career, I was asked to relocate and head up HR for the European business and manufacturing organizations for my US-headquartered employer. My prior knowledge of the business and some of the programs that were successful in the United States led to an effective partnership with the European organization and executive team. We accessed US programs and tools that made sense, modified others and still other times we used European approaches when it was the best option. I was also able to leverage my prior working relationships with key US counterparts to get quick answers or resolutions to move projects or business decisions forward. A five, eight, or twelve-hour time difference from other offices can often significantly slow down communications and decisions. Knowing who to go to and when and then having an already established relationship was immensely beneficial.

Motivating a Multinational, Multi-Generational Workforce

A multi-generational, multinational workforce is going to have varied expectations and be motivated by different drivers. A significant amount of my experience has been with fast-growing technology organizations where a large portion of the employee base is in their twenties and early thirties. In a nutshell, this generation wants to be heard and play an active part in not only determining what they do, but in deciding factors that affect the workplace around them as well. This is not only in the United States but globally as well.

In some countries (e.g. United Kingdom, parts of continental Europe, Scandinavia, India, etc.), business is traditionally conducted in a slightly more hierarchical way than the United States. You need to keep this in mind even when having high employee involvement and input into the business. Maintaining a sense of hierarchy in certain aspects of managing projects, decision making, and overall business communications is important to be effective in a number of these cultures.

Addressing other ways to motivate a multinational workforce involves understanding their various cultures and norms. We constantly endeavor to ensure that we are meeting local needs and expectations concerning compensation as well as benefits. This could include policies around time off and personal leave, which can be very different in other cultures and environments. We rely heavily on the knowledge of our local teams and partners so that we can understand how we might want to do something slightly or very differently in one of these offices because there are differing motivators and practices that are accepted for that region.

Developing Flexible Work Guidelines and Practices

I have worked in a number of organizations that allowed employees to work flexible hours and engage in other flexible arrangements. However, many of those practices either were not documented or not documented very well. This often led to confusion and inconsistent use. When we moved last fall from the suburbs of Boston to the downtown Boston waterfront, we understood that the move would affect our workforce in many ways, including time spent commuting to work. So we decided to establish and clearly document some consistent standards around flex time. First we researched employees' needs surrounding flexibility. Prior to that move, about 80 to 90 percent of our employees drove to work. However, now that we are in Boston, approximately 10 percent drive to the office, a very different dynamic than what we had previously. People, especially those with families who had other early morning or afternoon commitments, had significant concerns about how they would get to the office every day.

To be proactive, we formalized our flexible work policies around a variety of things, including start hours, hours of work, ability to work at home a certain number of days per week, and full- and part-time schedules. In the process, we really tried to ensure that these policies were not just accepted by subsets of the company but by the entire organization. At the same time, we instituted these policies in the United Kingdom and Australia. When we worked with our local partners in these countries to roll this program out, we found that it was uncommon to formalize these practices as policy. Many countries have statutory rights around certain aspects of flexibility, but our guidelines were actually broader than some of those. We really wanted to be forward thinking about granting people this flexibility because we thought it was very important, even in smaller offices. Now all employees are eligible to participate in these flexible practices after six months with the company—and approximately 20 percent of our total workforce does so.

Ongoing Listening to Our Employees

We recognize the importance of having a team that is not only contributing to the success of the organization but feels personally invested and passionate about their impact and contribution to that success. Because our focus is continuously on employee engagement, we leverage employee engagement surveys as one of the methods to gain insights. Then we follow up in a number of ways including small group discussions led by our senior leaders. From this input, we are able to plan companywide initiatives and strategies with active employee involvement.

These surveys and discussions provide the impetus for new initiatives and the ability to evaluate existing programs. They have led us to look at everything from our learning and development offerings to building out our compensation structure as well as piloting Dream Meetings, which I mentioned previously. After hearing that many employees were hungry for personal development and growth, earlier this year we closed down for a half day so that we could offer all of our employees, across the globe, a variety of developmental seminars and programs. Additionally, we have created Communispace University, which provides ongoing opportunities for our employees to learn from others both in and outside the company.

We have gained significant insight from surveys on what benefits employees most value. We have added and updated benefits to meet and/or exceed employees' feedback. This year, in the United States, we introduced benefit equalization for those domestic partners or same-sex married couples that participate in our benefit plans. While we previously offered domestic partner coverage, ensuring participants were not paying additional taxes than their opposite sex couple counterparts was important. Even though it did not impact a large portion of our workforce, we were interested to discover that it was an area that many of our employees really felt passionate about; they felt it was the right thing to do. We also launched a number of new wellness programs that offer everything from onsite exercise classes to information on healthy eating. As part of this initiative, we partnered with a local start-up organization around wellness assessment and development for all our employees globally.

The Importance of Acknowledging Individual Needs and Contributions

Overall, my experience has been that employee engagement and satisfaction stems from being open-minded and proactively supporting differences across your organization in addition to having key global programs in place. As a company, we understand the need to acknowledge what makes us each individuals—i.e., where we come from, what experiences we bring to the table each and every day, and what we are passionate about. Our clients and business partners reside across the globe; they are diverse in their backgrounds as well as their needs. It is critical that we are diverse as well and are able to effectively partner with them and provide significant value and insights no matter where they are.

Objectivity and keen listening skills are critical aspects to employee relations and HR overall. It is the ability to put assumptions and hearsay aside. This involves actively listening to your audience and working with both managers and employees to resolve issues and/or business problems. "The Grail" is often finding that balance between business needs/priorities and employee needs/desires. This can be a difficult balance to maintain at times. However, in all the successful businesses I have been in, employees are the "secret sauce" behind the product or service we are offering. Having fully engaged employees is a win/win for the business, its clients—and its employees.

Conclusion

Effective human resource leadership and programs are even more critical in today's business world and climate than ever before. Incorporating a global perspective and approach is an important way to ensure success for your employees, clients, and ultimately your entire business. This perspective or "global lens" can be used in everything from considering effective employee programs, communication channels, general practices, and company culture. Leveraging and listening to your leaders, business experts, and employees (no matter where they are based in the world) will ensure high employee engagement and business success moving forward.

Key Takeaways

- Continuously strive to create an environment and provide employee programs that support a thriving culture with high employee engagement and involvement.
- People listen and learn in different ways; it is essential to communicate messages using a variety of methods.
- When working with a global workforce, it is critical to listen and be sensitive to regional and/or cultural differences. Avoid immediately jumping to headquarter-centric views and/or solutions.
- In international offices, leveraging the knowledge of your local teams in conjunction with your business or industry experts is critical.
- When creating effective business and benefits programs, actively listen to employees to understand their needs and values.
- Objectivity and keen listening skills are critical aspects of employee relations, HR, and business overall

Barry Hartunian, chief talent officer and vice president of human resources at Communispace, has twenty-five plus years' business and human resources experience across a number of industries. Most notably, he has been an active business leader in the technology and software sector with companies that have experienced significant growth and success in their markets. He has a great deal of passion and experience in global HR, having lived and worked abroad, as well as successfully pioneering and growing the international operations for a number of companies.

Mr. Hartunian currently resides in both Boston as well as Provincetown, Massachusetts, with frequent travel within the United States as well as across the globe.

Dedication: *I would like to dedicate this chapter to my mentors, both formal and informal, over the years. I sincerely hope that I can have the same positive impact on my colleagues and team members moving forward.*

Navigating Employee Relations Issues During Organizational Transformation

Greg Kayata

Vice President, Total Rewards

Covidien

ASPATORE

Introduction

As the HR business partner for our global business unit, I work with a number of generalists who are aligned with the various divisions in the unit. In this role, I collaborate with my peers to establish our strategic direction as well as any deliverables that we agree to as a group. These deliverables are then put together at the corporate level by project managers in our centers of excellence before they are deployed throughout the business unit.

To provide an overview for this chapter, we are presently undergoing an HR transformation that is a result of a broader HR initiative related to our delivery model. While our employee engagement survey helps inform us of feedback, we are using best practice guidance as we revise how we deliver our services to the business.

Since we have recently gone through a series of acquisitions, and we plan to continue on this path, there is a significant amount of change management also involved in our work. We need to ensure that we onboard the employees from these acquisitions without disrupting the positive growth potential and successfully assimilate the different organizational cultures. It is important that we maintain the entrepreneurial spirit that is typically found in a smaller entity but sometimes gets lost in a larger organization. In essence, we must strike a balance and assimilate the groups without suppressing some of the richness that made those organizations so attractive to us in the first place. Employee communications is particularly key in this process, so we partner with our communications staff to ensure we are deploying a variety of communication vehicles, whether they are town hall meetings, skip level meetings or online surveys. These channels help us maintain two-way communication at all levels of the organization.

Moreover, we are working toward establishing a more inclusive environment by re-evaluating our talent management strategies, providing mentoring opportunities, and enabling diversity within our structure and daily interactions. The benefits of focusing on employee development at all levels are twofold: employees are encouraged to take ownership in their own developmental pathways, and each manager can more effectively understand how each employee enables development for the organization. We emphasize that development is a collaborative approach, and it is HR's responsibility to create the tools that will enable this collaboration.

HR's Development Model

The global business unit has been chosen to pilot a career-pathing HR development model, so we are focusing on making sure that individuals have robust development plans that are aligned with our new HR capability model. We also want to be sure that individuals are availing themselves to the offerings and experiences that would enable their development within this model. From an external sourcing standpoint, we are placing emphasis on diversity and inclusion, and we are trying to broaden our talent pool of qualified candidates so that we are casting a wide enough net. As part of that initiative, we are implementing behavioral interviewing modules to help provide us with a clearer view of our talent on a more proactive basis—understanding our talent from the outset, even prior to, the employment relationship. To that end, we will be in a better position to evaluate candidates early on and avoid dealing with certain challenges that may result from the wrong person being hired. Additionally, we are focusing on building manager capabilities to better capitalize on the potential of all employees in the organization.

Managing organizational development is somewhat of a challenge, because the direction of the business morphs a bit every time a new acquisition joins the organization. Consequently, we are doing quite a bit of work to support the changing organizational model while keeping a close eye on the bottom line. We want to make sure we create a sustainable structure; we certainly do not want to be replicating costs as we integrate these acquired companies.

Employee Relations Management

Employee relations concerns are, of course, managed on a day-to-day basis. In the United States, we have a designated support center that handles transactional and administrative responsibilities so that the employee relations staff can focus on tasks that require more subject matter expertise such as policy application or labor law issues.

The effect that employee relations has on the culture and overall health of the organization is actually a changing model for us. We have compartmentalized the responsibilities for the HR community, which involves making sure that managers and employees understand the personal benefit this model offers them. In other words, instead of supporting the business with a cadre of HR generalists, we will deploy specialists in the various HR disciplines such as employee relations, talent management, organizational effectiveness, recruiting, compensation, etc.

In parallel, we have deployed an HRIS platform that enables point-of-service support. This platform is intended to promote manager and employee self-service. We have received some feedback from concerned managers who feel they are doing work that has traditionally fallen under the umbrella of HR, so right now our primary goal is to help these managers understand where HR can add value to the business and where it is actually much more efficient for managers to take care of certain employee relations issues. We are trying to establish the fine line between staying connected with all employees while demonstrating that certain situations are best handled from a self-service standpoint.

In a general sense, however, addressing employee relations issues comes down to determining which circumstances are self-service appropriate and can be handled efficiently and promptly through the support center, and which issues would benefit from working with an HR specialist. This way we can determine which issues are unique and specific to our business in order to most effectively leverage the subject matter expertise of our specialists.

Managing Diversity and Inclusion

As previously mentioned, we are in the process of rolling out a few different corporate programs related to diversity and inclusion, but they mostly involve a central theme of building awareness. The process is about creating a framework at the corporate level and then encouraging employees to employ that framework in such a way that is most meaningful and applicable to the individual's unique work environment. We have found that this approach works well, and we have seen a number of grassroots efforts emerge at the local level. These efforts are particularly relevant and effective, because they are created by the employees; it is not something that has been prescribed to them from corporate. These grassroots programs also help us confirm that respect for cultural differences can be achieved at a very local and personal level. We developed these programs with sensitivities to cultural differences, and we are doing follow-up with participants at specific events to determine our success. For example, we recently brought in a speaker to address women's heart health concerns, which we followed with a survey to ascertain feedback about the event itself, as well as suggestions for future events. We want to make sure the programs we offer are resonating with our employees.

As for managing a multi-generational workforce, there is no one size fits all when it comes to applying HR solutions. There are certain administrative elements that can be directed to the support center, of course, but for specific concerns, the employee relations specialists are prepared to fully understand and appreciate the nuances of our employee population and address any unique individual needs. When dealing with different generations, it is important to recognize that employees will have different health needs as they age, and family profiles are going to evolve over time. It is important to address these different stages of the life cycle from a career planning perspective as well. Since there are a number of elements that change over the course of one's career, we try to be sensitive as people grow and evolve in the company.

Creating Work-Life Balance

Although work-life balance is something that cannot necessarily be prescribed as it is specific to an individual, we do have some general guidelines and policies to help employees achieve this balance. It can be quite challenging, especially when there are work-related responsibilities that must be accomplished in a given timeframe, but both the manager and the employee must show a certain degree of flexibility to ensure we are taking a holistic approach and recognizing all individuals as people, not just as employees.

Consequently, to help our employees achieve this balance, we offer flexible hours so that people have the option of working more hours on one day and fewer on another, if needed. During the summer, we also have early release on Fridays, provided those hours are made up during the balance of the week. We do have certain policies available, but by and large, a great deal depends on what the manager is willing to do to address an employee's specific needs based on the necessities of that particular office or department. It is virtually impossible to create one policy that will address everyone's needs, so we need to provide our managers with the skills to effectively address these concerns on a case-by-case and employee-by-employee basis.

Encouraging this flexibility is important, because it certainly affects the workforce morale; people need to feel that we care about them as people, not just as employees. When you create a unique and understanding relationship with your employees, you set the tone from a retention standpoint as well. Employee turnover often has a great deal to do with manager and employee relationships. If a manager is enabling a satisfied work-life balance, then you have a better chance of retaining that individual over the long term. A competing organization may have a more attractive pay rate, but if the work-life balance is not there, then the money may not be as attractive to the individual.

To monitor employee morale, we use an engagement survey that is taken every couple of years. We have also established, within our business, a vehicle that takes a core summary of those employee engagement questions every six months to discover if we are getting traction on any of our HR initiatives. These surveys help us determine what is going on from a morale standpoint and get a sense of whether our HR initiatives are appropriately engaging our employees.

Talent Development and Career Training

In addition to work-life balance, we also offer a broad spectrum of talent development and career training. These programs were created based on the notion that individuals are not going to get everything they need in the confined boundaries of a classroom. A large percentage of what happens from a developmental standpoint, 70 percent in fact, is developed from on-the-job experience. Consequently, we believe in enabling developmental assignments on a day-to-day level versus sending someone outside for classroom training. We also have online resources where people can take self-paced training, and we do have offerings where people can go into a classroom setting either here on campus or off campus. However, we believe the focus should be on the day-to-day exposure that employees get within their own roles rather than classroom training.

Effective Communication Strategies

When it comes to employee relations, effective communication is about striking the right balance: there is such a thing as too much information, and people simply cannot absorb it all. It is also important to remember that a large part of communication depends on listening; it is not all about broadcasting. Take employee feedback into account and make sure you are delivering information to them in a manner that they find relevant. Be receptive to what is appropriate for your particular audience. We have found that a multifaceted approach works best, so we hold town hall meetings, one-on-one meetings, skip level sessions, and regular staff meetings to address a variety of needs. Our strategy is a blend of what a manager does at a local level combined with things that are done at a business unit and corporate level. There are also meetings to address the general state of the company, as well as e-mail flow about various initiatives taking place.

Addressing discontent and conflict will certainly depend on the issue, such as whether it is global or local, or whether it involves a manager or a specific part of the business. Generally, it is a matter of trimming down to the lowest common area of concern and addressing it at that level. Solutions to sources of discontent tend to be very local, often personal. It is for this reason that the resolution needs to be owned at the manager level.

Common Errors in Managing Employee Relations

The most common errors in managing employee relations issues are usually a result of a lack of listening. I am a firm believer in understanding someone's personal context because no two people are alike. Along the lines of context, we owe it to ourselves as HR professionals to become present in the business, and well versed in the language of the business and its drivers. When HR rolls out programs without business context, understanding, and input, the result is usually a lack of credibility and a lack of relevance. For example, our business has various sales channels, touching a variety of customer call points for products that range all along the spectrum of the product life cycle. If we advocated for one sales incentive scheme for all of these channels, we would not be able to attract and retain the talent appropriate for each of the channels. Unless one understands the nuances of each of the channels, the respective markets, products, etc., you do not have the appropriate context, or corresponding credibility, to support the needs of the business.

Conclusion

Establishing credibility is critical to being a business partner in the truest sense of the term. This journey starts with learning about the business by listening, observing, and asking questions. Foundational to any effective HR program is the understanding of the business drivers. Like most businesses, ours is in a very dynamic market and competitive landscape. We are aligning our HR approach to ensure that we can best support our business in this environment. Part of this is helping to create sustainable productivity by delivering services in the most efficient manner possible. Another way for HR to facilitate the success of the business is to promote the development of global leaders and capabilities so that we may compete in the global marketplace.

Key Takeaways

- Encouraging diversity and inclusion cannot necessarily be prescribed at the corporate level. Create a framework to help guide your employees, but allow them to take the initiative at the local level in the development of these programs. This approach not only promotes local ownership but also enhances relevance to the target audience.
- When managing employee relations issues, remember that there is no one-size-fits-all approach. Encourage managers to be flexible and understand individual needs in order to create the most effective solution. It is important to consider the perspective of the employee in crafting a solution.
- Communication is essential in the role of managing employee relations. It is tempting to fall into the trap of "trying too hard" and pushing communications in quantities or media that will not be received by the audience. Listening is critical in this process, as is ensuring information is presented in a manner relevant to the individual.

Greg Kayata joined Covidien as vice president of human resources for the Vascular Therapies Global Business Unit in December 2006, bringing more than twenty years of human resources leadership to the role. Before joining Covidien, Mr. Kayata had a variety of business partners and center of excellence roles in Invensys and General Dynamics. Mr. Kayata completed his bachelor of arts degree in psychology from Providence College and his master of science in industrial relations from University of New Haven.

Driving Company Goals Through a Focused Employee Relations Strategy

Lyle Mark Daugherty
Vice President, Human Resources
Ancra Group Companies

ASPATORE

Introduction

My role in the organization is to serve as a business partner. I support multiple sites, working closely with our operations, but also with the management team on both short- and long-term objectives from a growth and profitability standpoint. My job requires being able to move quickly from a hands-on, direct role to somewhat routine things, and then being able to quickly shift over to a more strategic viewpoint. It could be as simple as conducting orientations to as complex as providing guidance on the right staffing levels after a merger or acquisition.

We are small enough to be very hands-on, interactive, and communications-based with our employee relations approach. We are also small enough at each of our sites that we can have close interaction with our employees each day to understand what is going on in their lives and to be able to communicate what is going on with the company. There is a lot of exchange regarding expectations and goals as well as feedback on what is going well (and not so well).

Managing Employee Relations

Our most prevalent employee relations issues involve keeping our employees current regarding market changes, helping them to understand where the competition is focusing their efforts, and explaining where we need to focus and improve our operations to keep up or stay ahead of them.

Employee relations certainly affect the culture and overall health of any organization. It is the foundation of how people are treated and valued in an organization and it sets a tone and leads to better engagement through reassuring employees that their contributions have high value. When you have engagement across the entire organization, you end up with an organization that is working toward a unified set of goals.

As a result, it is important to establish a positive culture for the organization. The management team must listen to ideas and provide support and time to encourage implementation of those ideas, because implementing ideas is an accelerant for more ideas. The people who are doing the work on the front lines will typically know and understand the best ways to solve problems, and it is a shame to waste their talent by not asking for their engagement.

Who Is Involved in Employee Relations Strategies

Of course, frontline management drives employee relations from a practical, day-to-day perspective. Our first-line supervisors are key because they are the closest ones to our employees' issues. They work with our employees closely, and they are the ones who can also represent the company to each of our employees. Our business unit heads are also involved in employee relations management to garner general philosophical support at the highest levels.

Preparing Managers to Be Effective in Addressing Employee Relations Issues

Depending on an organization's size, it can be complicated to effectively prepare managers to address employee relations issues. I have worked in organizations where it was much more difficult than it is here, because we had many sites and thousands of people and hundreds of supervisors to align. You need four or five key philosophical values at the core of your employee relations strategy, and those key values have to be understood by everybody in the organization. Most people can remember five things. If you boil it down to just those things, you can create consistency. Training is required to ensure a proper understanding of those key philosophical values, and to reinforce what behaviors reflect an understanding of those values, so that there is not a significant difference how each site approaches those values. Also, company goals need to be set and measured with those values in mind so that their importance are adhered to and demonstrate that deviations from those values will not be accepted.

The real key to training managers lies in improving their understanding of good communication. Oftentimes, there is a misconception as to what proper communication truly consists of. What you say, and the degree and level of detail you share is important. Employees will always tell you that they want to see communications improve. However, if you dig deeper into the issue on a very practical level, you will find that employees are actually requesting that we listen better to them. There is a reason why we have one mouth and two ears. If we listen twice as much as we talk, we will always understand better. When we listen, we can engage. When we engage, we find ways to capture the minds and hearts of our employees. That is when all companies are strongest.

Important Skills for HR Professionals When Addressing Employee Relations

HR professionals need to have a focus on the business' core competencies and goals. You hear a lot about HR folks being out on the floor, talking to employees, and that is good for creating a sense of comfort, approachability, and an understanding of what is going on in their jobs. However, an HR professional needs to understand what the key performance indicators are for their company—whether it is safety, quality, cost, productivity, or all of the above. When you talk to your employees, you should understand how they are doing based on those items.

Also, there are a number of key performance indicators that show success within the HR department. That may be headcount, turnover, overtime or your OSHA rate. Things that affect the way employees feel about the company. Monitor how those things are going. It is okay to have nice conversations with employees, and you should certainly do that, but keep an eye on safety, overtime, or absenteeism—the things that are important to the success in any HR department.

Best Practices for Managing Diversity and Inclusion in the Workplace

First, you need to have an overall philosophy and understanding of what diversity is. Of course, without a common understanding there will be confusion. Many people automatically think "diversity" means gender or race. Those are characteristics of diversity, but there are many other characteristics that reflect differences in each of us. Valuing these differences as an organization allows these differences to come out. Most leaders would recognize that where you have people who look, act, talk, and think the same way, you may have some success in the short run, but over the long haul, you will not be able to sustain success through such a narrow viewpoint. It takes some time to help an organization understand that diversity does consist of physical and social differences, but there are many things that make our workforce diverse. Understanding the value in those and ensuring that those are heard and valued is something that should be ingrained in our organization's culture.

Ensuring that the culture is open to diversity starts at a very simple level—by making sure diversity is reflected within your organization. You need to have faces, viewpoints, and differences that are actually visible, and that is tougher than it sounds, but it is a signal to everybody that the organization values differences. Larger organizations have greater opportunity because there are more hiring, promotions, and opportunities. It is tougher in smaller organizations. At the very least, differences in opinion need to be valued. You can very quickly shut down engagement by minimizing any differences or ideas.

Effectively Managing Employee Relations with a Multi-Generational Workforce

There are clearly some real differences in values between generations. I am in my late forties, on the fringe of the boomers. There are people in our organization that are the same age as my kids, in their late twenties. What each group values is different, so policies and programs need to allow flexibility for those differences. Flexibility itself tends to be very important for younger generations. Policies need to consider things like stability and security for our older employees. By ensuring both flexibility and security are clearly visible in your organization, both generations see that you are considering what is really important to them. Periodically, you have to stop and evaluate your workforce. What does it look like? What are the demographics? What are their needs and are they changing? I would encourage this reflection every five years or if there are significant changes to the organization. Stop and review your policies and your practices to see if they still match up with your employee demographics. Ask what is effective for this time. Have a mechanism for employee feedback. Let your employees express concerns or ideas about how policies should be adjusted, value their feedback, and where it makes sense make changes that reflect the inclusion of your employee's ideas.

Different Employee Needs Based on Generation

To simplify things, let us just divide the generations between the younger and older set. It is not that simple, but it is an easy division. The younger employees look for flexibility and more immediate opportunities, whether that is training and development, promotion and growth opportunities, or a flexible schedule. But there has to be consideration given to what I will call stability and security items. Older employees appreciate this. That group has seen many changes, ups and downs in the economy, layoffs and job losses. Programs that enable them to prepare for retirement, provide for their kids or grandkids, and pay off their mortgage make them more comfortable. There must be recognition by HR of the different needs and the usefulness of creating programs around those differences.

The other generational change I have seen is in candidate selection. Candidates provide a very different profile today than we received many years ago. Part of that is the economy. That is an opportunity—make sure that when you have an opportunity to hire, you can understand the differences existing between candidates.

Recognizing the Differences in Candidates

Applicants today have more job changes on their resume. When you conduct background checks, you will probably see more small or minor offenses. Years ago, you did not see that, or you had the ability to select around that, because worker availability was different. If you wanted a candidate with steady work history, you would not have a problem finding that. Now it is more difficult because of the changes in the level of unemployment. Even within the last three or four years, so many people have moved around and taken jobs that do not match their past work history.

Back in the early '90s, when we were staffing the big Toyota plants, we could be selective. We rarely saw anyone with a DUI or marijuana possession. We would automatically take them out of the running. We would not even consider them. The selection process has since changed because the workforce has changed.

Work-Life Balance Factors in Employee Relations Strategies

Work-life balance is especially important for companies that are in a very competitive labor market whether it be lower, unemployment or what you are paying is average for the market. If you are offering a job that does not differ much from the job down the road, you need to find ways to be different. Allowing flexibility when somebody needs to come in late or leave early is a significant benefit. Maybe adjust the work schedule for people to allow for childcare or to pick them up or drop them off during the school year. Be sensitive to the personal obligations your employees have. If you are small enough to do that, it matters and is easy to do. On the other hand, if you work in a big company, it is much more difficult. You need clear policies in place that consider those needs, whether that is a reduced work schedule, a part-time schedule or flexible start and stopping time. It is harder to be flexible because there needs to be an established policy.

Ensuring Employees Receive the Right Messaging and Understand Protocol

Making sure employees get the right message and understand how to route questions depends on the frequent visibility of HR professionals with their employees. Formalize in your mind the ways that you will get in front of employees, whether that is your daily schedule or lunch box meetings or small group discussions. Make sure that there are methods to allow people to talk with you face-to-face. In addition, set up documented or best practice ways to make sure that opinions are gathered, whether that is opinion surveys, suggestion systems, or other kinds of employee engagement tools. These are all ways to make sure that opinions are heard and concerns are raised. There are methods in union plants with grievance procedures to voice concerns about unfair treatment, but you can also have other concern resolution processes without having a union. When there appears to be inconsistent applications of policies, allow people to write down their concerns and have it reviewed formally. That can lead to change. When you demonstrate that change can happen, your employees will be more likely to tell you if something is not going right.

Monitoring Employee Morale

There are a number of ways to measure employee morale. The most common is to do some sort of periodic opinion or employee survey on key things that are important to your company. If you have established four or five key values in your company, you can then ask questions that are founded around those values to see how you are performing.

More important than doing a survey is the actions that come as a result. Involving employees in a solution to their own concerns is great for engagement and boosting morale. When you ask the question, "How would you like to be involved in addressing this?" nine out of ten employees will be willing to get involved however they can. But one in ten will say no, and explain they just wanted to let you know. Maybe it is actually not that big of a concern, but if they are raising it, there probably is a real reason that you should be paying attention to.

Formalize your method for requesting employee feedback on a periodic basis. Just make sure it is regular so that employees feel it is a focus and so that you can measure any shifts.

Identifying Discontent

Identifying whether there is discontent, and if in fact there is discontent, it is important to understand the source of the discontent. If it is a production concern or operations concern, you obviously have to involve the people who can make the decisions to improve the situation. But it is good to involve your employees who have some ability to impact and change others' understanding of what the real problem is. This may be an HR person who has a good relationship with all the departments.

Not every issue is a sky-is-falling kind of thing. You have to understand which issues are a big deal and when discontentment is growing, and rally the groups of people surrounding it for a change. Some management employees you do not want to involve because they could add to the discontent or be the source of the discontent. However, if they are the source, they have to understand how they are contributing to the problem and ultimately make some adjustments. Having a relationship with the various departments is very important for HR to be a closer business partner and not just an audit function.

Staying Abreast of Legislation

The most important laws and regulations for employee relations are the obvious ones that are rapidly changing and associated with the National Labor Relations Board (NLRB). Based on the administration in place in Washington, things swing greatly as it relates to the NLRB. So it is important to keep up. There have been many changes over the years as far as employee involvement and union organizing. Employee relations and labor relations are described differently but they are still the same. It is how you treat the people you work with.

Conclusion

Knowing who you are as a company and what your key operating philosophies and values are should be engrained in every business action and decision that is made. The foundation upon which your philosophies and values are built should be one of two communications. Ensure that your employees understand what they are doing but more importantly why they are doing what they are doing. This will give you the best opportunity to engage your employees.

While there are many short-term gains that can be made through directing or demanding employees to do things, this method cannot be sustained in the long haul for any company. Management's key role is to set a direction for success in the organization, communicate those goals and methods to all employees, and create an environment where ideas on how to reach the goals are welcomed and each employee can contribute as fully as possible to the organization's goals. Most companies value their resources tremendously, and in this day and age, most technology is available at a price. When it comes to being a leading company, the main difference will not be capital, technology or a trade secret, but the organization's people. We should learn that and live that philosophy if we want to be a leader in our industry.

Key Takeaways

- When you have engagement across the entire organization, you end up with an organization that is working toward the overall goals together, and you have a more satisfied workforce as a result.

- Implementing ideas is an accelerant for more ideas.
- Your first-line supervisors understand that they are the company in the eyes of their employees, and their actions will speak most loudly to your employees.
- Differences in opinion need to be valued. You can shut down engagement by minimizing differences or ideas.
- When there appears to be inconsistent applications and policies, allow people to write down their concerns and have it reviewed formally. That can lead to change. When you demonstrate that change can happen, folks will be more likely to tell you if something is not going right.
- More important than doing a survey is the actions that come as a result. Involving employees in a solution to their own concerns is great for engagement and boosting morale.

Lyle Mark Daugherty, vice president of human resources at Ancra Group Companies, is a human resources professional with nearly twenty-five years of experience working with Global Fortune 500 companies.

After receiving his undergraduate degree in business administration and master's degree in industrial and labor relations from West Virginia University, he began his career at PPG Industries working at two locations, including being part of the start-up team for a new facility in Berea, Kentucky. After working over three years at PPG, he was recruited away to Toyota's first wholly owned and largest facility in Georgetown, Kentucky, initially in employee relations. During his nearly twenty years of working with Toyota, Mr. Daugherty had the opportunity to work in every aspect of human resources including being part of the management team at both Georgetown and in Erlanger, Kentucky's North American Manufacturing and Engineering Headquarters. During that time, he had the privilege to participate in numerous start-ups and lastly to lead the human resources department for one of Toyota's largest Tier I suppliers, Toyota Boshoku America. In 2011, Mr. Daugherty moved to work for a division of the Heico Companies, the Ancra Group Companies, and has since been involved in that group's key leadership team and participated in multiple site mergers and acquisitions and in improving the group company's competitive position in the marketplace.

Managing Generational and Cultural Employee Relationships

Melissa Dunn

Global Director, Human Resources

Thermo Fisher Scientific

ASPATORE

Introduction

My current role is as the global director for human resources within the Thermo Fisher Scientific's organization, which is a $12 billion organization with more than 38,000 employees globally. Thermo Fisher is a global leader in the science field with products that are designed to make our world cleaner, safer, and healthier. At my level, we are considered strategic within the business model. HR works side by side with the business leaders to form strategies, make decisions, and perform actions that affect all levels, making HR an integral part of our organization.

Employee Relations Management

Employee relations management has two sides to it: one is what I call the administrative side that ensures that routine questions regarding benefits, policies, and the like are handled in a timely and efficient manner. Our organization is very large and spans across many countries so to help manage the administration of such a large company and to remain consistent we have an internal website (intranet) called "iConnect" which provides a wealth of information, including all of the necessary forms for our benefit programs. Our intranet is also a learning tool with many podcasts and interactive programs available on various subjects including human resource topics. The second side of employee relations is being a resource to employees, specifically management in order to guide them in effective management of their people. Retaining and building talent is really our number one job. If you are doing well, then we want to be able to help develop you as an employee, we want you to be identified, and we want to ensure you are being challenged and fulfilled in your career. If you are not performing, then the behavior or actions need to be performance managed. Within large companies such as this, sometimes it is easy for people to get lost, but HR needs to work with the business managers to actively manage our people to ensure that we have the right talents in the right jobs.

Active employee relations are essential. Most importantly, employees want to feel that they are needed and respected and that they are making a contribution. The overall organization benefits when the managers interact frequently with their employees. Communication is essential, especially when a company is experiencing cultural changes. Regular interaction gives employees the feeling that they are working in an inclusive environment where issues will be heard and addressed. It also allows management to set the tone to drive a growth and performance culture.

Facilitating Positive Relationships

There are a variety of ways to facilitate positive relationships both internally and externally. The internal strategy consists of a great deal of training, some of which is driven locally and from the corporate office. The employees who undergo internal training are chosen because they have been identified for their interest in learning specific areas. We also have mentoring programs that allow employees from every department to learn about working in all areas of our organization along with developing skill sets from a mature business perspective.

Externally we contribute a great amount to the community both in time and programs at charitable events. There is always some type of event to get involved in which allows people to work together. One way our employees interact is through our gardening project. We have a full garden where people can get a piece of land garden during the spring and fall. You can keep the fruits of your labor for yourself or donate all or in part to a local pantry. We are very proud of our Community Action Counsel. A variety of programs are part of our corporate culture including regular food drives, wellness programs, involvement in numerous charitable events, etc.

Developing and Maintaining Employee Relations

While my position is involved in the development and maintenance of employee relations, it is the executives who are most involved, as it is a top down process. The top down process ensures that all levels of the workforce are committed.

To ensure regular communication with our business leader I have regular one-on-one update meetings with senior team members. I do not wait for them to come to me—I go to them. We meet at least once a month, if not more, and we do what we call "taking the temperature" where we go over what is happening in each area. In one area, we may know that we have many retirements on the horizon so we need to know what our plans are to manage this change in the team. We may also need to discuss our talent and focus on our high potentials. Retention is very important as talented employees can always find another opportunity with another organization.

Preparing Managers to Address Employee Relations Issues

To make sure that our managers are prepared to address employee relations issues we have monthly training for newly hired managers. This training gives managers the skills they need to address and handle employee relation issues along with an understanding of our policies and the company philosophy regarding people management. We have a variety of management leadership tracks for employees. For some they may be on the professional track that focuses on being an individual contributor in their field where others are groomed for larger leadership roles. It is the company's responsibility to give these employees the tools they need to be successful in their careers. Our intranet (iConnect) is a very useful tool, especially for new managers who can choose various podcasts on leadership, conflict resolution, ethics, code of conduct, etc.

Talent Development and Career Training

We have an entire team dedicated to talent management at our organization. Any employee can go online through iConnect and really choose to train for a variety of subjects. If you want to learn a new language, we have Rosetta Stone, which you can take for free. We are not only encouraging education for your job but for your own personal development as well. Through iConnect there are entire learning modules and portals. As the largest science organization in the world, we feel that the education and development of our employees is an important aspect.

There are several tracks for career-based training. There is management training and technical training as well as the training outlines that we create each year as part of employee goal setting. Training can occur in a variety of ways. It can be web based or it can be in person with an in-house trainer. Thermo Fisher is a training focused company with constant training through many different venues.

Mentoring Program

To determine who should be involved in our mentoring program we begin with our annual human resource review (HRR) for all of our talent in the organization. We decide at that point who may need a mentor to get them to the next level. The mentoring program is a great way for managers to be rewarded and recognized. Mentoring is a learning process for both parties. This decision process occurs each year and then the program details are recorded and monitored. It is important that the company stays abreast of the outcomes of our mentoring process.

Essential HR Skills

The most essential trait for an HR professional is common sense, along with the ability to know the business and relate to people. HR professionals are not personal counselors or police officers. Unfortunately, I have encountered these types of misguided HR professionals throughout my career. It is sad to say but some of the worst managers I have met over the last twenty years are in the HR field. The police officer way of doing business is the old HR model. On the opposite end, I have interviewed young students who want to be an HR professional because they want to help people. I tell them that they should become a social worker and that an HR professional is a business partner, not a personal counselor. I tell current up-and-coming HR employees that success is all about good common sense. Be discerning and get to know people and the business; be that business partner your executive team needs.

Top HR Mistakes

The top mistake HR makes is that they think they are the center of the universe and do not look and learn beyond their own department. We are a critical support function to any business. HR is a functional role with the primary goal of offering tools and assistance to our leadership to effectively manage their talent. Many HR departments keep themselves separate and are not sitting at the table and being actively involved. Another big mistake of HR is being too passive. In HR you have to have thick skin and be willing to rock the boat if necessary. Being passive and putting blinders on regarding poor performance and behavior hurts the business in the long run.

Best Practices for Managing Diversity and Inclusion

A part of the overall corporate goals and the HR goal tree is diversity. We are reaching out to community action groups and various organizations to ensure job openings are made available to a wide range of individuals regardless of gender, color, and disability. Our company employs many different diversity initiatives and a month ago, we hired a diversity director whose job it is to ensure that there is diversity among the 40,000 people who work for Thermo Fisher. Diversity is important but I do not believe in achieving it by hiring to fill quotas. We are trying to get our name out in the community so that a diverse group of candidates will feel welcome to look for career opportunities in our organization.

Cultural respect among our diverse employees is important. Diversity training is available to all managers. During my career I have performed cultural sensitivity training and coaching. It is also essential that the work environment is an open place where if someone feels they are being singled out due to their cultural differences they feel comfortable enough to speak up.

Managing Employee Relations across Generations

Managing relations with employees of different generations presents its own set of challenges. I think the younger generation of employees is focused on the idea of "What are you going to do for me?" along with work-life balance. You must understand that they are not driven by money or the things that used to drive previous generations. When I am dealing with the younger employees, it is important to show them why their actions have affected specific outcomes. Quite often young people do not see how their behavior/actions affect the result. When dealing with younger employees we must help them understand that we are not their moms and dads. I have actually had to say that to employees during my career. I explain to our employees that we want them to have a positive work environment where they can come to work and feel fulfilled but at the end of the day we need them to perform and fulfill their job responsibilities.

The main motivation for the younger generation is a balance between work and life as well as training; they want to be educated along with ensuring they have work-life balance. At my previous employer during the recession in 2009, we had to reduce workweeks down to four days a week. Once we could bring back a five-day workweek we thought people would be so happy to start getting paid for a forty-hour work week. But that was not the case because the time off was more cherished than losing one day of pay for over six months. This is a different generation where time is more important than money; they want time to play sports, continue education, and spend time with family and friends.

The older generation has a more focused work ethic. An issue we face with older generations is that they have been here a long time and they are used to the way things have always been—the famous "remember the good ol' days." Therefore, we must help them with the change process. That is where many employee relations issues in the older generations arise. The employees may have been poor performers for many years and no one has addressed it, or they are struggling because they cannot deal with the changes in the workplace, specifically technology, and the pace of doing business.

Sometimes there is no easy way to help employees deal with change, especially when the organization is going through numerous changes in a short period of time. Leaders must be ready and willing to communicate changes in a timely and effective way. For some it needs to be made clear that change is not optional. In these cases, employees need to decide if they are dedicated to making this work and in essence willing to get on the company bus. Either way the bus will be leaving the station. Some just simply do not get on-board. Helping employees understand and explaining that "Yes, this is the way it was, but this is the way it is now and here is why" aids older generations in dealing with changes. Explaining the why is critical.

Work-Life Balance Factor

Work-life balance is of great importance. The company gives people a reasonable amount of vacation time each year and allows employees to take one paid day a year to participate in a charitable activity of their choice. The company is sponsoring a charity event called "Take a Stake at the Lakes." Over eighty volunteers from our facility will participate in cleaning the lake shores in our town.

Flexible schedules are important as well, especially in the summer. During the spring and summer, we have a program that allows employees to work extra hours Monday through Thursday so they can get out at noon on Friday. Work-life balance is important.

Following Legislation

I get regular legislation updates, but in addition to that, I get two legal updates—one federal and one from the state. I follow legislation not only locally but also globally as I am interested in overseas legislation, what is currently happening in France and China, and changes in employment law. I follow China's employment law closely because it changes overnight.

Essential Laws and Legislation

The essential laws and legislation depend on what region you are in, but anything that has to do with employment contracts is important. For instance, in 2008 China passed a law that when employer contracts are up and if they are renewed by the company the employee in essence has a "forever contract," making it very difficult to downsize any employee. A law recently passed in the United States has made unionization easier. It is important to look at changes to all laws that we are currently following to determine if any company policy changes need to be made. For instance, we might need to update our posters. We pay close attention to pending legislation especially now during an election year

Communicating with Employees

Our internal communication process begins with identifying the needs of the employees involved, and then goes to an outline form that is sent to the first tier of management and onto people like myself, as well as the executive leadership tier, then onto the corporate office. This is all done to make sure that the right message and proper wording are being expressed to ensure that the message is meeting all the audience's needs. Quarterly town hall meetings are also an important venue for communication. These types of events are televised globally. There is also an avenue to utilizing technology via the iConnect site to field questions and submit comments. Technology based communication such as webcasts, teleconferences, e-mail, instant messaging, communication boards, etc., are incorporated throughout the entire organization.

If an issue is performance based it is communicated directly to the employee from the beginning. If an employee has a concern and they do not want to come directly to the person the issue concerns, HR is the first stop and then there is an escalation process.

Monitoring Employee Morale

It is impossible to continuously monitor employee morale, but we do surveys every other year to measure it. The information from those surveys might reveal a variety of things such as how people feel about development, how they feel about their training, and potential employee needs. We also have daily and weekly meetings to gauge what is going on.

I like to listen to the people who I call "the centers of influence." They can be anybody in your company, it does not matter what their titles are, but they are employees who people listen to. These employees are easy to identify based on their natural leadership abilities as well as their communication skills. Sometimes these centers of influence lead to a gossip mill that needs to be halted. However, listening to the word on the street usually gets to the heart of the matter.

The major warning sign of employer relations issues is when you start to hear rumors of things that you know people are making up. When employers do not have enough information and we are not communicating effectively, then people will make up their own reality. You can tell this is happening through lack of participation, absenteeism, and fast turnover rates.

Conclusion

At the end of the day, people are separate individuals with different needs and wants. Therefore, it is impossible to manage a business or its people with the one-size-fits-all approach. It is an opportunity or challenge, depending on how you want to look at it, for the HR professional to first recognize this truth. Communication methods need to be adapted to meet the needs of all people. It is our role to understand and apply the right method, and it make take more than one approach. There is no doubt it will involve some trial and error.

Employee recognition and engagement can occur in many ways. It can be done formally or informally. HR needs to help company leadership understand and manage various employee motivators and assist in creating the right methods that work in each environment. Embracing diversity and understanding there is more than one way to skin a cat is very important. Utilize best practices internally and externally. Stay involved and make connections—there is always some organization that has encountered the issues you are facing. The final key is accepting at times that you may not have the answer and say so, and then make your own path in discovering one.

Key Takeaways

- An effective HR professional needs to possess common sense and a commitment to understanding the business.
- Be honest and do not expect to have all the answers.
- HR professionals are not police officers, nor are they therapists.
- Clear communication is essential on all levels to maintain employee morale and prevent the spread of rumors.
- Different generations of employees have different motivators and concerns.

Melissa Dunn has eighteen years of human resource professional and executive management experience and is currently responsible for the global HR function as a global director within Thermo Fisher Scientific, a publicly traded global organization with more than 38,000 employees and $12 billion in annual sales. Ms. Dunn specializes in union negotiations (domestic/internationally), employee relations, strategy deployment, talent management, mergers (demergers)/acquisitions, executive recruitment, global relations, management coach, strategic planning, and organizational development and training.

Ms. Dunn has experience in overseeing HR structure and deployment for multiple locations in the United States and around the world. She has experience managing the

HR *process in Sweden, United Kingdom, Germany, France, Italy, China, and India. Her key responsibilities include driving deployment and execution of global* HR *initiatives, policy development, union/labor negotiations (domestic/international), legal compliance (domestic/international), resource development, executive recruitment, leadership and organizational development, management training programs, and corporate benefit/pension administrator.*

Ms. Dunn's past positions include group vice HR *president at Concentric AB (global manufacturer—publicly traded in Sweden), vice president of* HR *and labor relations at BHCCU, and multi-divisional* HR *manager at Kerry Ingredients (global food and food ingredient company—publicly traded in Ireland).*

Tailoring the Right Employee Engagement Strategy for Your Organization

Kelley Berlin
Senior Vice President, Human Resources
SymphonyIRI Group

ASPATORE

Introduction

SymphonyIRI Group, Inc. (SIG) is the leading global provider of innovative solutions, services, and integrated empirical information on markets, consumers, and shoppers to enable CPG, health care, and retail companies to dramatically increase revenue, build brands, and improve productivity. We employ more than 3,500 full-time employees worldwide.

As the senior vice president of human resources (HR), my primary responsibilities include developing and implementing the overarching human resources and talent management strategy for each business function. I also lead the talent acquisition strategy, including all the strategy, process, and tools required to successful hire the best talent from the market and meet the staffing needs of the business.

Setting Strategy and Employee Engagement

One of the company's key strategies during the last few years has been to transform our go-to-market client model with the goal of creating greater value for our clients. This strategy has affected almost all of our people programs. The focus has been on creating high value for our clients by providing business insights that drive greater business performance for clients.

When I first starting writing this chapter, the focus was on employee relations, but as I reflected on what they really mean at SIG, I realized that a more appropriate way to describe this is by discussing the key employee engagement strategies that create the highest levels of employee satisfaction.

By having a clear strategy that is well articulated, understood by the employees of the organization and supported by the leadership team, employees will be more likely to have a high engagement level.

Within SIG, we work hard to drive the highest level of engagement with our people, focusing on how we connect employees with the broader SIG culture and strategy, especially given our decentralized workforce.

Connectedness in a Decentralized Environment

The more connected employees feel, and the more ownership they have in the vision and values of the company, the more engaged they are in the company. This leads to higher retention and productivity and overall satisfaction.

Many of the employees at SIG work on-site at our clients or work virtually, so our challenge and focus is on keeping our employees connected to our company culture and brand. We are unique in that many of our employees actually sit on location at many of our client sites. We are often challenged with how to keep them connected to our company culture and values even though they are really at a different employer's worksite and are exposed to that company's culture and values.

Finding the Right Tools to Connect Your Workforce

As the world becomes more virtual and technology driven, we lose face-to-face interaction, which draws people in and connects them, so it is harder to keep our employees connected to the company culture/brand. We are experimenting with various approaches to meet this challenge.

We are piloting a new tool within our organization that we have named PeopleConnect. It is a social media tool almost like our own internal Facebook. We have named it PeopleConnect to do just that. As a real-time Facebook type tool, it allows us to connect employees in a different way across functional groups, various employee levels, and multiple geographies.

PeopleConnect allows for sharing of best practices on a specific topic or functional area. Groups have been created to focus around specific business issues or questions and then a selected group of users can follow the content, as they would on Facebook, to learn about these topics and share context or engage in a dialogue. Users post information, chat, ask questions, and share presentations. They can post video clips of themselves, which is great not only for new hires, but also to allow all of us to feel more connected by attaching a face to a name.

Another way we are exploring to better connect employees in a more intimate way is through town hall sessions on a smaller scale. In addition to the traditional companywide town hall meetings, our leaders are hosting smaller, more personalized meetings with fifteen to twenty people and creating a conversational format. The first five to ten minutes typically include standard content about the vision or business results or a critical initiative within the company, and the remaining time is spent in a Q/A format, which promotes an open dialogue and discussion with the goal of gaining a connection with employees.

Creating and Implementing Strategy with the Executive and Management Team

Our executive leadership team is responsible for creating the business strategy for each of their business units. The HR team provides the underlying structure for those business strategies through a talent plan that supports and enables execution of the strategy. There is an ongoing dialogue between the business leaders and the HR business partner supporting the business unit to determine the talent and other resources required to implement the various strategic initiatives. Once these strategies are agreed upon, communication to the broader organization is driven at the business unit level, meaning it is each leader's responsibility to ensure their employees know and support the strategic vision and plan for their area.

To ensure that the business unit strategic plans are aligned across the organization, we also host an annual senior leadership team meeting early in the year that is a two-day strategy session for our top fifty leaders across the organization. During this meeting, each executive presents the strategy for their business segment, and the group discusses execution and implementation of these initiatives.

The strategy and progress against the strategy is updated throughout the year through formal and informal meetings and various written communications from our leaders.

How well we deliver this information to employees has a direct link to their understanding of the strategies, which, in turn, affects their overall engagement toward the company.

The Most Important Skills for HR Professionals

Human resources' skill sets have evolved tremendously during the past five years. Today's professionals require a much higher level of strategic planning and thinking skills.

The most crucial skills for a great HR professional include the following:

- **Excellent communication skills:** Must have finely tuned written and verbal capabilities to communicate at all levels within the organization.
- **Outstanding client relationship/partnership skills:** Great HR leaders build strong client relationships and become true business partners to the leaders in the organizations that they support.
- **Viewed as a trusted advisor:** Ability to understand the policies, procedures, and values of an organization, and really work with the leadership team to build strong relationships. This expands the sphere of influence and creates a bigger need for the HR function. That is where true value is added.
- **Unbelievable organizational and multitasking skills:** The volume and the level of content coming at us in any given moment is huge, so we need to be able to work on many different tasks at different levels, and engage effectively with all of them. The key to this is being able to prioritize those items that have the biggest impact to the company while still getting the broader HR work done.
- **Think creatively and be innovative:** In my view, HR's added value comes from thinking outside the box. Maintaining great employee relations is important, but we also need to think about the next generation of HR. We need to ask ourselves how we can continually evolve the value that we bring to a particular organization, leader, or employee team and accelerate our ability to drive the overall strategic plan of the organization.

Learnable Versus Natural Skills

I am a firm believer that many, if not most, HR skills can be learned and developed over time; however, great HR professionals have an innate ability for sound judgment and good intuition that are not as easily learned. This, coupled with the skills above, is really what differentiates a great HR leader from a good HR leader. Having great mentors and seeing people who do these things well will significantly accelerate the learning curve.

Talent Development

We are launching a new talent development portal in the next six months on our intranet site that offers many tools for employee development. It gives employees a holistic view of how all the pieces of development fit together and includes a number of tools to assist them, such as how to prepare to have a conversation with their managers, how to build on that conversation and develop that into an action plan. This helps them to actualize the skills needed for development. The portal also has online classes, classroom-type programs both inside our company and outside through partner organizations, and reading resources based on particular competencies. Through this site and a supporting communication strategy, we hope employees will take more accountability to increase their awareness of the different tools and resources available to them and take action around their development planning.

Best Practices for Communicating Effectively

Currently, we rely on broad e-mail communications supported with webinars to share best practices formally and informally. Leaders host lunch and learn trainings or informal sessions on key topics that we want to share. Over time, we hope to move toward an online communication system and further leverage the PeopleConnect tool mentioned earlier.

Monitoring Employee Morale

While we have not conducted a broad scale employee engagement survey in some time, we plan to do so in August to ensure we are working on improving the engagement levers that have the biggest impact on our company's ability to achieve results and drive employee engagement. This will be the first large-scale engagement survey that we have conducted in many years. Up until now, we have focused on engagement surveys focused at the department level, and while these have been helpful and very targeted, we feel the timing is right today for a broader companywide process.

Addressing Employee Morale Issues

To address morale issues, we engage the leadership team for that particular group and dig to find out how much we really know about the issue. Do we need to get more information? Do we have enough knowledge to put an action plan together? We further dissect the situation to ensure we have full understanding of the issue and the true root cause. In some cases, we may interview a few employees to get their perspective. Then we build an action plan around the issue and a communication process to see if we can help bridge the gap. Leadership plays a large role in engagement with our employees, and we hold our leaders accountable for retaining, engaging, and motivating local teams.

The Top Mistakes of HR Professionals When Dealing with Employee Relations Issues

Professionals in the early stages of an HR career make too many assumptions too soon in the employee relations process. They often do not take the time to keep an open mind and to make sure they have a real assessment of the situation. We hear one or two things that seem consistent with a theme, and we jump on that versus really dissecting and assessing. We need to do that and then go beyond to get to the root cause of the issue. HR professionals sometimes jump to conclusions too quickly and do not address the true business issue.

Tracking Legislation Related to Employment and Labor

We track legislation around employment and labor, but we rely on our legal department to keep us informed of anything that is changing. Also, within our compensation and benefits organization, we have a policy management process. They are always checking to make sure that we are in compliance with different regulations or legislation.

Ensuring Alignment between the Changing Business and Employee Strategy

On the tactical level, we do not plan to make any changes in the near future around employee relations and management. On the strategic level, we always look for ways to keep our employees engaged and connected to our business. New technology and a virtual environment means there will always be new initiatives to really keep employees branded and focused and aligned with their core company culture. I cannot really predict what those will be yet, but my guess is that the need to connect employees will keep growing year over year.

The HR team goes through a strategic planning process once a year. We look at various business units and their strategies, and then we look at our HR strategic agenda. We match those up with business strategies to ensure that we are addressing the company's biggest priorities. Our HR business partners rely on their relationships with division leaders to ensure that strategic agendas and programs are aligned with overall business objectives for that unit.

Conclusion

Human resources can significantly impact the overall employee engagement level by ensuring clear strategies are put in place and well communicated by the leadership team. They can also educate the leadership team of the benefits of putting actions in place to promote a high level of employee engagement so they understand the linkage between employee satisfaction and business results. As organizations continue to create virtual work environments, ensuring employees feel connected and engaged with their organization becomes more challenging. Leaders will need to continually look for new creative ways to keep employees engaged given the changing dynamics of the communication tools available and constantly changing workforce environment.

Key Takeaways

- The more connected employees feel, and the more ownership they have in the vision and values of the company, the more engaged they will be.

- Connectedness is a challenge in a decentralized environment. Look for tools that promote interaction and sharing.
- An HR professional needs to be viewed as a trusted advisor and business partner who understands the policies, procedures, and values of an organization, and works with the leadership team to build strong relationships.
- Excessive movement out of a particular group or business unit can be an early indicator of morale issues.

Kelley Berlin, senior vice president of SymphonyIRI Group, joined SymphonyIRI in July 2002. She is responsible for executing SymphonyIRI's talent strategy for the US business. Her focus is on providing superior human resources solutions through strategic partnerships and innovative practices by promoting change, empowering employees, and driving business growth and innovation. This includes providing respectful, efficient, and effective services to all employees, creating a work environment of trust, empowerment, and satisfaction in support of SymphonyIRI's strategic advantages, its people, and their capabilities.

Ms. Berlin possesses more than eighteen years of experience in achieving superior human resource results. Prior to joining SymphonyIRI Group, she served as the director of human resources for Moore North America (since acquired by RR Donnelley), where she led the human resources strategy for the US organization. Prior to Moore North America, Ms. Berlin served as director of human resources for The Registry Stores Inc., a start-up retail venture. She began her career with Montgomery Ward. Ms. Berlin holds a bachelor of science from Northern Illinois University and masters of business administration.

Dedication: *This chapter is dedicated to my husband, who is my rock and soul mate in life.*